Living Free

Living Free

How to Live a Life of Radical
Freedom and Infectious Joy

Steve Brown

A Raven's Ridge Book

Baker Books

A Division of Baker Book House Co
Grand Rapids, Michigan 49516

Published by Raven's Ridge Books
an imprint of Baker Book House Company
P.O. Box 6287, Grand Rapids, MI 49516-6287

Printed in the United States of America

Library of Congress Cataloging-in-Publication Data

Brown, Stephen W.
  Living free / Steve Brown.
    p.   cm.
  "A Raven's Ridge book."
  Includes bibliographical references and index.
  ISBN 0-8010-1094-2
  1. Christian life. I. Title.
BV4501.2.B7669   1994
248.4—dc20   94-31529

Unless otherwise indicated, Scripture references are from the New King James Version, Copyright © 1979, 1980, 1982, Thomas Nelson, Inc., Publishers.

Contents

Introduction and Acknowledgments

This book is a companion to *Born Free* and will continue with the material our ministry, Key Life Network, offers in our "Born Free" seminars. It also contains some updated material from my book, *No More Mr. Nice Guy.* Much of this book is taken from the actual transcript of the seminar and, along with *Born Free* and another book coming out next year, *Being Free,* will read a bit differently from my other books.

Some Christians are a "pain in the neck." This book is not designed for them to become better at it. Christian boldness is another "critter" altogether. It is the grace of God in the life of the believer who is secure in the unconditional love of God and, thereby, is free to speak truth boldly, to laugh freely, to forgive quickly and to make a gentle and uncompromising witness to the fact that we are great sinners with a great Redeemer. Christian boldness is an attitude that comes from a relationship with Christ. It comes from free Christians who don't have a hidden agenda, who no longer have to prove a point, who are not witnessing to their own goodness and who no longer have the need to be right.

Someone has described the church as a nice man or woman standing in front of nice people, telling them how they can be nicer . . . and I'm afraid that our Christian witness is going to die from "niceness." Christ didn't die to make us "nice." He died to make us free. In that freedom is bold love, bold obedience and a bold witness. Christian boldness is a reflection of Christian freedom.

This is the plan, a road map, as it were, of our journey to boldness. In chapters 1–3, we are going to take some time to define terms and to outline a biblical philosophy of boldness; in chapters 4–6, I want to talk to you about some of the things that keep Christians from being bold; and finally, in chapters 7–8, I want to give you some practical "how-to" material.

Before we begin the journey, I must thank some people who made this book and the "Born Free" seminar possible. (After all, what good are friends, family and colleagues if they can't share some of the blame?)

First, I want to thank my wife, Anna, who models unconditional love, whose wisdom and balance keep me from going off the "deep end" and whose strong support and encouragement have always been a "rock" in my life. I want to also thank Robin DeMurga who did all of the editing and piecing together of the material in this book. Robin is our daughter and edits much of my written material. (Because she loves me, Robin makes sure that I don't say stupid and embarrassing things and, most of the time, is reasonably successful.) I want to thank my friend, Steve Griffith, who represents Key Life Network to publishers and who has more ideas for me than I could possibly fulfill in ten lifetimes. Cathy Wyatt, Key Life's Vice President of Marketing, has been responsible for the general oversight of all the "Born Free" seminars and is appreciated more than she knows. Richard Farmer, Key Life's Executive Vice President and one of the dearest friends I have, makes sure everything works and the bills are paid. (He has kept me out of trouble and, probably, jail.) Thanks to the staff, board and volunteers of Key Life who make what I do possible by "holding up my arms." Also, I must say thank you to my colleagues and friends at Reformed Theological Seminary in Orlando, Florida, where I teach, who keep me reasonably orthodox . . . and, especially, to the President, Luder Whitlock, whose encouragement and support of this somewhat radical (critics have said "weird") Christian is a major grace gift from the Father.

I wish you could have the experience of a "Born Free" seminar where the music of Buddy Greene and the drama of Ruth and Charlie Jones ("Peculiar People") enhance the pedagogical enterprise. The material I teach is a lot better when those dear friends are around to help.

It is my prayer that this book will make you so bold and radical that "uptight" and "bound" Christians will doubt your salvation.

1

Poor Presumptions

Stereotypes of a Saint

There are two basic traps we, as Christians, often fall into: the traps of perspective and manipulation. These traps keep us from becoming free and bold before the Father and before one another. It is important, therefore, that we first define the problem before getting to the solution.

The Trap of Perspective

What the World Thinks of Us

When the world thinks of Christians, it thinks in terms of a stereotype. The Christian stereotype: a bland, nice, quiet, insipid, agreeable saint. That makes me so mad I could spit!

Have you ever noticed how "objective" historians have conveniently deleted any reference to the Christian motivation of men and women in our past when that reference didn't fit their stereotype? Columbus, for instance, is seen as a courageous explorer with no mention of the fact that he was an explorer with the goal of furthering the gospel of Christ to hasten the date of the Second Coming. We know about Washington's false teeth, but no history book includes his prayers or his commitment to Christ. Hardly anyone, except in passing, mentions the Evangelical roots of almost every social reform in America. Wilberforce is a name most secular students of history never hear, and if they do, they don't know his deep commitment to Christ and the Christian roots of abolition that eventually swept from Wilberforce's England to America. Conversely, while Jonathan Edwards is perhaps the finest philosophical mind America ever produced, he is remembered only for his sermon, "Sinners in the Hands of an Angry God" (a very good sermon, by the way). His presidency of Princeton and his great philosophical works are simply ignored. (Edwards's *The Freedom of the Will*, published in 1754, is a superior sampling of his philosophical writings.)

A number of young, single women in the church I once served had a constant problem with the passes they got from young pagan males. They told me it is difficult to convince a pagan that they simply aren't interested. I suggested to a number of them that they give the man making the pass a mini-testimony of their relationship to Christ. Subsequent to my suggestion, a number of them came back to me and said, "It worked like magic. I waved the wand of Christ over his head and he disappeared!"

While that is an effective way to deal with the unwanted passes of pagans, I am disturbed when I think of why it may be so effective. It could be that no red-blooded American boy wants to be associated with a Christian woman because he has a stereotypical image of her that is somewhat less than flattering.

In a very critical review (one with which, incidentally, I disagree) by Aram Bakshian, Jr., of the *Mr. Rogers' Neighborhood* program, Mr. Bakshian writes:

Mr. Rogers is the perfect neutral babysitter. A kindly, chinless person with grey hair, grey jacket, grey sweater, grey trousers, and, for all I know, grey undergarments, he addresses his youthful charges in a nasal bleat that makes George McGovern sound like Macho Man by comparison. Since he also dubs voice-overs for all of the puppet characters, the aural impression, like his personal color scheme, is uniformly bland. The premise of the show, shaped in part by two "psychological consultants" whose names are run with the credits, seems to be that hyperactive young Americans need nothing so much as a daily aerial lobotomy, presided over by the unmenacing May-Bap figure embodying the virtues of a kindly granddad and a particularly unassertive schoolmarm . . . By the time Mr. Rogers discards his tennis shoes and sweater and heads for the door at the end of each thirty-minute installment, one can't help suspecting that the brighter kids in the audience breathe a sigh of relief refreshed with the certainty that, for a merciful 24-hour interlude, "Mr. Rogers' Neighborhood" has gone with the wimp.[1]

With a few minor changes, Mr. Bakshian's comments about Mr. Rogers could be the comments of the average pagan talking about a Christian. The stereotype the world has given to Christians is nothing less than frightening. When anyone becomes a Christian, given that stereotype, it is even more a miracle of God's grace than the Bible says it is.

A young couple came to see me once with a request that I perform their marriage ceremony. There was a problem. She was a Christian, and he was not. In fact, he had no interest in becoming one. I explained to them that the Bible placed on me a certain obligation about the kinds of couples for whom I could perform the marriage ceremony. I told them that I could marry two Christians and I could marry two pagans, but that I couldn't "cross-fertilize" (see 2 Corinthians 6:14–15). And so I explained to them that I was prevented from performing the ceremony. Then, to my horror, the young woman began to cry. If that was upsetting to me, you should have seen her fiancé.

This big, bad pastor had hurt his future wife, and he was really ticked. He rose up to his full six feet three, clenched his fists and said, "Reverend, I thought the church was here to help people; I thought you were here to keep people from crying, not to make them cry." Then he took his future wife's hand and pulled her out the door. (To be perfectly honest with you, I was glad to see them go. He was mad and he was big. I'm not a wimp, but I'm not stupid either!)

I was thinking about that incident later, and I decided that his view of the church, though obviously wrong from a biblical standpoint, was nevertheless the view held by many people. If they don't hate us, they, at least, think that we're a relatively benign institution set apart to "hatch, match and dispatch." It is no wonder that, as Christians become involved politically, there are such loud protests. Face it, it is just not politically correct to be a Christian!

A lot of folks who have become so angry about Christians in the public square have come to their hostility because they thought they had Christians figured out. Christians are supposed to be "nice" and "insipid." Well, the pet kitten over in the corner turned out to be a lion. When a kitten roars like a lion, has claws like a lion and has teeth like a lion, you don't want him on your lap—you want him in a cage.

Not too long ago, I was in a meeting between the editors of our local newspaper and the religious leaders in the community. It was a meeting designed to help us understand each other. One of the editors, in trying to explain the newspaper's position, said, "We don't go after the church in a news story unless the church does something outside its traditional role."

I was angry, and before I had a chance to put on my smiling clergy face, I was talking. "Are you telling us," I said, "that you will leave us alone as long as we keep our place; but if we do something that doesn't fit your preconceived idea of what the church does, we will not be okay?"

To be perfectly honest with you, his words sounded to me like the words of a racist telling blacks that as long as they dance, sing, play the trumpet, eat watermelon and keep their place, they will be okay. The editor, of course, denied that that was what he meant, but I have no doubt that his "Freudian slip" was showing.

I believe that Christians who have moved outside the walls of their militarily-defensible church buildings and into the public square are hated, not only for the things for which they stand, but because they aren't supposed to stand at all. They are Christians, and Christians are supposed to be seen and not heard; Christians are supposed to stay in church, smile and talk about God; Christians are supposed to bless the mess of paganism and act like a kept woman.

Unless you have been hiding under a rock somewhere, you are aware of the unfortunate stereotype of Christians in our society. It is the stereotype that files Christians under the heading "Wimp."

What We Think of Ourselves

The wimp stereotype makes me angry, but let me tell you something that makes me sad: We Christians have often been the ones to create the stereotype and we have then tried to conform to it. In other words, the horrible thing is that, in some ways, the world's pathetic stereotype of us is the same as our stereotype of ourselves.

It is important what the world thinks about us, but far more important is what we think about ourselves. I am not too concerned with what the world thinks about Christians. I am, however, very much concerned with what we think about ourselves. We are called to be bold believers. Any change in that direction has to start at home—with how we see ourselves.

Someone tells the story of the eagle egg that somehow got into a chicken coop. The mother hen realized the egg was somewhat larger than the other eggs; but after all, she was a mother so she sat on it. The eagle hatched and, for weeks, played the chicken game. The eagle knew he was different; he knew that the other chickens thought he was different and they only tolerated him. He tried to eat off the floor of the chicken coop like the other chickens, but it never felt right. He tried to walk like a chicken, talk like a chicken and squawk like a chicken, but he could never quite pull it off.

Sometimes the eagle would look up in the sky, wondering what was on the other side of the clouds. He would say to his fellow chickens, "Don't you ever wonder what's up there in the sky or what's on the other side of the mountains?" The other chickens would look at him as if his elevator didn't go all the way to the top. But the eagle trapped in the chicken coop never stopped wondering and asking questions.

Then, one day, the eagle looked up in the sky and saw a speck. The speck grew larger and larger until the eagle realized that it was a creature like himself—an eagle. He heard the creature call loudly, and the call echoed against the chicken coop. At that moment, the eagle knew he wasn't a chicken. He knew he was an eagle. He flapped his wings and began to fly. Soon he was soaring above the clouds!

The problem with that eagle wasn't just that everyone thought he was a chicken. The eagle's real problem was that *he* thought he was a chicken. Something like that has happened to Christians. Somehow we have gotten the idea that being a Christian means being a wimp. It isn't true; but if enough people tell you that you are a wimp, you'll start acting like one. That can be overcome . . . if you know the truth. If you don't know the truth, however, you can end up in the prison of the chicken coop for the rest of your life.

So, there is the Christian stereotype. The question now is: How did the stereotype develop among Christians themselves? It is my thesis that Christian boldness doesn't happen because we don't believe that Christian boldness *should* happen.

Let me give you some Scripture important to this discussion. The first passage is Proverbs 23:7 in which the writer admonishes believers to stay away from certain people because "as he thinks in his heart, so is he."

Philippians 4:8 teaches:

> Finally, brethren, whatever things are true, whatever things are noble, whatever things are just, whatever things are pure, whatever things are lovely, whatever things are of good report, if there is any virtue and if there is anything praiseworthy—meditate on these things.

The psalmist, when he asked God to "check him out," said, "Search me, O God, and know my heart" (Psalm 139:23). And Paul, in telling the Christians at Rome to be transformed, said, "Be transformed by the renewing of your mind, that you may prove what is that good and acceptable and perfect will of God" (Romans 12:2).

The point is this: What we think about the world, and especially what we think about ourselves, will inform and mold our actions. If Christians think that being a Christian means being weak, insipid and bland, then we will be weak, insipid and bland. Not only that, but if enough of us think it, we will give the impression, both to the world and to those who have just become believers, that Christianity is weak, insipid and bland. Eventually, the lie will become the reality.

The Trap of Manipulation

Perspective is not the only trap. The second trap we need to be aware of is the trap of manipulation. An important warning: Beware of those who will attempt to manipulate you. With that end, I want to expose the three lies that lead to "yes." Contrary to popular opinion, "no" is not a dirty word.

"No" Is Not a Dirty Word

Charles Spurgeon was fond of telling his students, "Learn to say 'no.' It will do you more good than Latin." He was right. But, as a matter of fact, most Christians simply don't know how to say "no" to anything that sounds religious or which carries the adjective of "Christian."

We understand that a Christian is to say "no" to practices that are "no-nos" in the Bible. We are called to say "no" to temptation; we are not to be engaged in sexual immorality, drunkenness and lying. Christians are to say "no" to the devil, to false gods and to false men. The Ten Commandments give us a number of "thou shalt nots," and we are very clear on them. The problem with most Christians is not that they don't know how to say "no" (though we often don't) to bad things. The problem is that we haven't learned to say "no" to good things when we should.

I do a substantial amount of travel in my speaking and have noticed in nearly every place I have gone that most committed Christians are tired. They are tired simply because they operate out of the spurious notion that Christians are supposed to do everything that anybody tells them to do if it is Christian.

I have a dear pastor friend who has many talents, but one of his best talents is taking up an offering. He used to conduct large youth rallies; and, every time I attended those rallies, I decided before I went what I was going to put in the offering, because I knew that, if I waited until I got there, I would end up giving everything I had in my pockets.

My friend would often say before the offering, "Look around you. The odds are that you are sitting next to a nonbeliever and that nonbeliever is watching you. In our country, you can tell what a person believes by looking at his checkbook. What is that nonbeliever going to think if you only put a dollar in the offering plate? I'll tell you what he is going to think: he is going to think that you don't really believe it, or that you only believe it a dollar's worth."

At other times, he would say, "If you had gone to a movie tonight it would have cost you five dollars. You add to that the dinner and the gas money and you are up to twenty-five dollars. Do you love Jesus as much as a movie, dinner and car fare?"

By the time this man finished his announcement before the offering, I had opened my billfold, taken everything out and dug into my pocket for all my loose change too. I want you to know that I simply could not let Jesus down in my witness to the pagan next to whom I was sitting . . . and I certainly loved Jesus more than a movie!

One time, my friend was away on vacation and asked me to conduct the rally. I tried some of his "techniques" when the offering time came up and I thought I had done quite well. After the rally, I went to the back room where the offering was being counted and found myself rather proud of the fact that there had been a good offering. I commented to the secretary who was overseeing the counting that I felt we had done well. She smiled and said, "Yes, it isn't bad, but Jack (not his name) would have gotten twice as much!"

The Three Lies That Lead to "Yes"

The offering taken by my friend is a good analogy of how Christians get manipulated into saying "yes" when we ought to say "no." Let's analyze some of the reasons why we say "yes" at the wrong times. It is usually because we have believed three lies.

Believing God Always Wants a "Yes"

First, we say "yes" when we ought to say "no" because we genuinely believe God always wants us to say "yes." There is a great lesson to learn in John's account of Jesus' raising of His friend Lazarus from the dead. You will find the incident in John 11:1–6:

> Now a certain man was sick, Lazarus of Bethany, the town of Mary and her sister Martha. It was that Mary who anointed the Lord with fragrant oil and wiped His feet with her hair, whose brother Lazarus was sick. Therefore the sisters sent to Him, saying, "Lord, behold, he whom You love is sick." When Jesus heard that, He said, "This sickness is not unto death, but for the glory of God, that the Son of God may be glorified through it." Now Jesus loved Martha and her sister and Lazarus. So, when He heard that he was sick, *He stayed two more days in the place where He was* (italics mine).

When Jesus finally got to Bethany, Lazarus was dead. Martha, the sister of Lazarus, gave Jesus a reprimand: "Then Martha, as soon as she heard that Jesus was coming, went and met Him, but Mary was sitting in the house. Now Martha said to Jesus, 'Lord, if You had been here, my brother would not have died'" (vv. 20–21). Later Mary, from whom you would have expected more because she understood Jesus better, was just as upset as Martha. "Then, when Mary came where Jesus was, and saw Him, she fell down at His feet, saying to Him, 'Lord, if You had been here, my brother would not have died'" (v. 32).

The interesting thing about that whole episode is that Jesus was in tune with God's agenda. He didn't care about everybody else's agenda. If we had been there, we would have said to Him, "Jesus, don't you care about your friend? He's sick and you can help. Yet, all you do is sit here." If we had been there, we would have told Jesus that His "Christian duty" demanded that He do something. We would have told Him that no Christian ever turns away from any need. "How can you say 'no,'" we would ask, "to such a great need?" And, if we had said that, we would have been absolutely wrong.

Let me give you an important principle: Immediate need is *not* God's call for immediate action. God's call for immediate action is the *only* call for immediate action.

One of my dear friends is Cleve Bell, the director of Riverside House in Miami, a ministry that deals with people while they are in prison and also works with them after they're released. Every time I'm around Cleve, I feel guilty that I'm not doing more in prison work. After all, Jesus said (Matthew 25) we ought to visit the prisoners. Sometimes, I get so guilty that I go with Cleve to one of our jails. (I have a similar feeling when I'm around Chuck Colson. I sometimes go with him too.)

A number of years ago, Jim Green (who is one of the most effective youth workers in the country), Eddie Waxer (who has a great international sports ministry), Cleve Bell and I had lunch together. Cleve was telling us about what God was doing in the prisons. Then, because he had another appointment, Cleve had to leave lunch early. I said to Jim and Eddie, after Cleve had left, "Don't you guys sometimes feel that we ought to be doing more of what Cleve is doing? His commitment to those prisoners puts me to shame."

Jim and Eddie were on me like "ugly on an ape." Eddie said, "Steve, have you ever had any indication that God has called you to prison work?" I allowed that I didn't, and then Eddie said, "Steve, if you aren't called to that work, stay away from it. All you will do is fail to do what God called you to do, and mess up what He didn't call you to do."

Jim said, "Steve, I pray for Cleve and support his work, but God gave me a burden for kids. I'm going to do what God told me to do." They were right, and I was wrong.

In Calvin Miller's first volume of his delightful Singer trilogy, the Singer (Jesus) had encountered a miller who was filled with pity because of his great pain and deformity. His arm and hand were scarred and had become practically useless because of an accident. The Singer offered to help, and the miller replied, "It cannot be so easy, Singer. Would you wave your magic wand above such suffering and have it all be done with? . . . Stop your mocking. I am a sick old man whom life has cheated of a hand. The nightly pain has already now begun. The Season of my hope is gone."

And then the miller fell on the floor and moaned in a great spasm of pain. Miller wrote, "His surging pain caused him to cry, 'O God deliver me from this body . . . I never can be well and whole as other men.' He waited for the Singer to join him in his pity, but when he raised his head for understanding, the door stood open on the night and the Singer was nowhere to be seen."[2]

Just like the Singer, we will come to places where we simply have to turn away. These are places to which God has not called us either because the situation doesn't fit into His plan or because the circumstances do not call for our involvement. The Singer could not help the miller because the miller's self-pity required anyone who would help, including the Singer, to participate in his pity. That was not on the Singer's agenda.

The point is this: Find out what God has told you to do and then say "no" to the rest. One of Satan's greatest tricks is to get us off God's track. There are a multitude of reasons why God would have us do one thing and not another (e.g., He is teaching a lesson, He has someone else chosen to do the job, He is working out a greater good, and so on). You see, God is the great chess Master . . . and He is the only one who sees the whole board. We are to play the part the chess Master would have us play and trust that He knows what He is doing.

Let me take an aside here and say a word about how a believer can know what it is God wants him or her to do. There are a number of good books on the subject of determining God's will; so, I don't want to take time for a detailed analysis of the subject. However, I have four principles I follow in that determination. First, I look at Scripture. The Bible is the only absolute guide to what ought to be the direction of my life (see 2 Timothy 3:16–17).

Second, there are circumstances. Ecclesiastes 9:10 says, "Whatever your hand finds to do, do it with your might." I believe that where I am is where I'm supposed to be and what I am doing is what I am supposed to be doing, unless God, who is perfectly capable of letting me know, tells me otherwise.

Third, there are the spiritual gifts God has given. It is clear that God has not called me to sing, given the fact that I sound like a fog horn (see 1 Corinthians 12:4–31 and Ephesians 4:1–16).

Finally, there are my brothers and sisters in Christ who love me enough to tell me the truth. Others usually are able to see my gifts better than I can. For that reason, I am always open to their input concerning the direction of my life (see Ephesians 5:21).

Believing "No" Will Hurt Our Witness

The second reason we say "yes" when we ought to say "no" is that we are afraid of what people will think. There is probably nothing in this world that will kill a Christian faster than constantly being on stage before the world, playing to an audience who will determine whether we are good, pure or faithful.

Thomas Kelly, the Quaker contemplative, emphasized this point in his work *A Testament of Devotion:*

> But there is something about deepest humility which makes men bold. For utter obedience is self-forgetful obedience. No longer do we hesitate and shuffle and apologize because, say we, we are weak, lowly creatures and the world is a pack of snarling wolves among whom we are sent as sheep by the Shepherd . . . If we live in complete humility in God, we can smile in patient assurance as we work. Will you be wise enough and humble enough to be little fools of God? For who can finally stay His power?[3]

There is probably nothing worse than a constant "acting out" of what we think of as a witness to the world. As a matter of fact, we are witnesses to what Christ has made of us, not to what we pretend to be. When we get those confused, we become true hypocrites.

Have you ever heard pagans refer to Christians as hypocrites because Christians are not good? I hear it all the time and I realize how miserably we have failed in communicating what the gospel of Jesus Christ is all about. A hypocrite is one who proclaims with his or her words or life what he or she doesn't believe. When a pagan says, "Those Christians are hypocrites because they pray on their knees on Sunday and prey on their neighbors the rest of the week," they simply haven't understood the gospel. If I should say that the Christian faith is for good people, call myself a Christian, and then am not good, I am indeed a hypocrite. However, that isn't what the Bible teaches at all. The Bible teaches that Christ came to save sinners—not good people. Therefore, my witness is not to my purity, kindness and love—it is to Christ's purity, His kindness and His love.

If your witness consists of your purity, those who know you will legitimately call you a hypocrite; and those who don't, will think that the Christian faith is only for good people. All you will see of them is their "heels and elbows" as they run in the opposite direction.

Is goodness a witness? Of course it is, but only the goodness that Christ gives the Christian; and when He gives it, it is never arrogant and judgmental. Is absolute goodness a witness? Impossible! "No one is good but One, that is, God" (Matthew 19:17). If our sin can't be used as a witness as well as our goodness, we have a serious problem.

I have a friend who recently became a Christian. She failed miserably in her sexual relationship with a young man who saw nothing wrong with having sex with anyone who was willing. "After all," he said, "it is just a normal need like eating and exercise. How could it be wrong?" My friend fell for that type of idiocy and then came to my study sobbing her heart out. I listened to her confession. Then, I reminded her of the reason Christ died for her.

Next I said to her, "Joan, you have a great opportunity to witness to this man. Why don't you go to him and ask his forgiveness for having betrayed the most important person in your life—Jesus?"

She did it and he didn't know how to handle it. She went to this man and said, "I want to ask your forgiveness. Sex is a beautiful thing and I can't say that I don't enjoy sex; but last night, I did something far worse than sleep with you. I failed to be faithful to Christ who loves me. I gave lie to the central belief of my life. I'm forgiven and things are okay between Christ and me, but where I really failed was in not showing you clearly about Christ. When I slept with you last night, my greatest sin was in hiding Christ. Will you forgive me?"

Now, that man is not a Christian because of her witness, but he is thinking about it. She had become one beggar telling another beggar where she found bread, and that was a whole lot different from one actor telling another actor where he can do some more acting.

What people think about God is not dependent on you or me. If you get to thinking that, the God you worship is not the God of the Bible. He is an idol you created who is weak and helpless without our efforts to help Him along. The God of the universe will be praised and honored because this whole thing is His show and not ours. So forget about the act. The world and God can do without it.

To be perfectly honest with one another, we are not so afraid of what the world will think about our God as we are about what other Christians will think of us. That, by the way, is what "cultural Christianity" is all about. We take what the Bible says about being a Christian, overlay it with what we "mature" Christians think about being a Christian, then we go and try to force other Christians into the mold we created. May God forgive us!

One time, as I participated in a Wednesday evening prayer meeting at the church I served, one of the "mature" Christians gave testimony to what Christ had done in his life. He talked about being delivered by God's Spirit from a number of sins. The next day, I had lunch with another man (a new Christian) who had attended that prayer meeting. After the chit-chat was over, he said to me, "Pastor, I've decided to leave the church." I asked him why. And he told me that he was never going to make it. He said, "Pastor, I listened to Bill last night, and I just don't have what he has."

I am bound by the secrets people tell me, so I couldn't reveal what I knew about the man who had given his testimony. But I said to my new Christian friend, "Listen, the first thing you have to learn about the Christian life is not to take too seriously what some other Christians say in testimony meetings. You say you don't have what he has. Well, he doesn't have what he says he has; and, if he were a little bit more honest, you could get about the business of the Christian life without trying to be something you're not."

Isn't it terrible that I have to tell a new Christian he shouldn't take too seriously what people say in testimony meetings? But you and I both know it's true. The church ought to be a fellowship of people who are terribly honest. The reason we aren't honest is that we are playing a game called let-me-show-you-that-I'm-a-good-Christian and the game is killing a lot of Christians who have left the fellowship because they simply couldn't play the game anymore.

Am I saying that Christians ought to be as bad as they can in order to be as honest as they can? Am I saying that we ought to amend the old hymn to read "I am sinking deep in sin; and, isn't it fun?" Of course not. If you can't say, with John Wesley, that you are "moving toward perfection," you ought to wonder if you are the genuine article. If you don't see Christ making you more loving, kind and compassionate than you were last year, there is something seriously wrong. Purity and holiness are important; but, if you have to fake it for either pagans or Christians, that sin is greater than the lack of purity. Let God worry about what the pagans and the Christians think—you worry about what God thinks.

Believing We're Responsible for Everything

The third reason we say "yes" when we ought to say "no" is that we believe the lie found in the oft-quoted cliché, "If you aren't a part of the solution, you are a part of the problem." That, when you think about it, is a dumb statement. It presupposes that, by not being a part of the solution to the problems of the world, you have somehow caused them. Such an idea is pure nonsense (and, before I was a Christian, I had better words to describe it).

I am not a very good house fixer. When something goes wrong at our house, my wife calls someone to fix it before I see it. After over thirty years of marriage, she has learned that, if I touch it, I'm going to make it worse. Do you know the best thing that I can do to make things run smoothly at our house? I can stay away from whatever is broken. What is often a simple and inexpensive repair can become, with a little help from me, a major "budget-busting" expense.

A lot of Christians have not learned that about life. Sometimes the best solution is to leave a problem alone. Have you ever met those Christians who feel that, every time there is a broken marriage, it is their responsibility to fix it? In most of those cases, they grease the tracks to the divorce court. May God save us from "do-gooders" who have absolutely no belief that God is capable of fixing anything without their help.

I do a lot of counseling and I am not a counselor. However, after over twenty years as a pastor and radio Bible teacher, I have learned, slowly, some important lessons. The hardest part about counseling is learning to be quiet when God is doing something important. I am an encourager. God has given me the gift of being a cheerleader for other Christians. Because that's the way I am, I have a tendency to want to put Band-Aids on cancer rather than doing the hard surgery. Time after time, after listening to a problem, I have wanted to say, "Don't worry. It's going to be okay." I am learning, however, that when God is doing surgery, I am not to interfere. In other words, I am learning to trust God.

You can't say "no" to good things unless you have learned to trust the sovereignty of God. It is only because He is God that I can sleep at night. Bill Schaffer, the former director of music and the arts at the church I once served, one time, told me after a very pressurized time at the church, "Steve, if I didn't believe that God was in charge of all of this mess, I would jump off the nearest bridge."

There are so many people in the world who will try, sometimes without meaning to, to manipulate you. They are everywhere; and, for that reason, you have to be careful—the television preachers who tell you their ministry is going to come tumbling down if you don't send money; the committee chairman who thinks that, when Christ returns, He will come first to that committee meeting; the religious leader who has a tendency to get a willing horse (a Christian who says "yes" all the time) and ride him till he dies; the parent who tells you that you couldn't possibly be a good son or daughter unless you call eight times a day; the social activist who makes you believe you are personally responsible for every social ill; and, even sometimes, the author (like me) who makes you feel you have to say "no" all the time.

Learn to say "no" to the manipulators. If you don't, you will never learn to be obedient to the only One before whom you are always required to say "yes"—God Himself.

Now, you need to know that everything in this book will be wasted . . . that is, unless there is a way to put it into practice. How do you deal with a bad stereotype within yourself? How do you deal with those who would manipulate and control you? I want to give you an important biblical principle, and then I want to draw three implications from that principle.

The Principle of Control

The principle is called the principle of control. It works like this: *Your mind controls your actions and emotions; your will controls your mind; you control your will. Therefore, you control your actions and your emotions.* When the Bible tells Christians to "think about these things," it presupposes that you have decided or, at minimum, *can* decide to think about them. The reason the Bible is so insistent on thinking about certain things or renewing your mind is that your mind and the attendant thinking process are the very center of everything you will become.

I spend a lot of my life on airplanes, and flying is my second favorite activity in the world (the first being to jump off tall buildings!). At any rate, a while ago, a friend who has a private plane took me to a speaking engagement. Once we were up and flying, my friend took his hands off the controls and said, "Steve, it's all yours!" I just about died.

"Jim," I said, "unless you are prepared to meet thy God, you had better take control of this thing. I refuse to touch it." My problem was that my friend gave me control and I didn't want it.

A lot of us are like that about life. We really don't want the responsibility for control. Mary McCarthy has said, "Bureaucracy, the rule of no one, has become the modern form of despotism." We don't like to be in control simply because we don't like to be responsible. I believe the reason we have committees is that nobody wants to make decisions, to take control and to be responsible. So we spread it around. The point is that you can't escape responsibility, at least for what you think and what you do. Your mind controls your actions and emotions; your will controls your mind; you control your will. Therefore, you control your actions and your emotions.

You Are What You've Decided to Be

Now, let's draw some implications from the principle. First, you are, at this moment, what you have decided to be. When Joshua renewed the covenant of the people with God at Shechem, he said, "And if it seems evil to you to serve the Lord, choose for yourselves this day whom you will serve . . . " (Joshua 24:15).

We live in an age in which perverted psychology has reduced people to the status of computers. If a person has not been programmed properly, we are told, he will manifest aberrant behavior. He is not responsible for what he does; he has no choice but to act as he has been programmed. The need, psychologists will say, is to take a "sick" person and to simply reprogram.

That approach would just be silly except that people have come to believe that, whatever they really are, is the result of how they were "potty-trained" or of the self-image given to them by their parents. We are a nation of victims. Murderers are not bad people; they are maladjusted people. Child molesters aren't to be punished; they are to be understood. Thieves have not done anything wrong; they simply have a correctable psychological problem.

Someone tells about a man who was sitting on a tack, and it was hurting. A psychologist came along and said, "Sir, the reason you are hurting is rooted in a childhood trauma. You need therapy." A sociologist then came along, saw the hurting man, and said, "You've got a problem, and it is obviously the result of the kind of environment in which you grew up. Hurt is from an improper environment." Next, an economist came along and said, "Money is the root of all hurt. Let me help you with your portfolio." Then a minister came along and said, "If you learn to praise the Lord in all your circumstances, you won't hurt so much. Your spiritual life leaves something to be desired. Start reading your Bible and praying every day, and it will get better."

Finally, a little girl came along and said, "Mister, why don't you get off the tack?"

One of the great discoveries of my life, as a pastor, was the discovery that people are what they have decided to be. We do things for what seem to us, either consciously or unconsciously, to be perfectly logical reasons. Most of the time, when someone is depressed, that person has decided to be depressed. If someone is a "pain in the neck," most of the time, that person has decided to be a "pain in the neck." With few exceptions, we are what we have decided to be. People are not computers. We are volitional beings; we make choices; and those choices determine what we become.

You Can Change

The second implication of the principle of control is this: Not only are you what you have decided to be, but you can also be different from what you are.

Recently, I talked to a young man who said he came to me because he needed help. He told me he had some friends who had become a bad influence in his life. They liked to go to a particular club where there were plenty of drugs, and even though he had promised both himself and God that he wouldn't do it anymore, he couldn't help going there with his friends. The young man said he had tried everything, but nothing seemed to give him the strength he needed to stop taking drugs with his friends. He expected me to give him some Scripture or some magic formula that would help him.

I said simply, "Son, why don't you stop?"

"I can't," he replied.

"What do you mean you can't stop? You're the one who goes there. Nobody forces you. You're the one who takes the drugs. Nobody puts a gun to your head and makes you take them. So just stop."

The young man smiled and said, "You know, nobody ever put it to me that way."

Three weeks later, the young man called and said, "Pastor, you gave me the best advice I have ever received. You said to stop and I did. I haven't touched drugs since I talked to you."

Now that may seem silly to you. You thought pastors had some kind of secret formula. You thought we could pray over problems and they would go away. But, as silly as it sounds, no one thought to tell him to simply stop what he was doing. Twenty years ago, I would not have had to tell him he should stop. Then, everybody knew that we decide what we are and, as a result, are what we have decided. It is an indication of how far our society has come down the road of complete helplessness that I had to tell him to make a choice. (I do not mean by using this example to minimize the difficulty of breaking a serious drug addiction. But in that situation, too, the person must begin by making a basic choice to stop using the drug, even if following through is painful or requires the help of others.)

It is my hope, as you read this book, that you will gain insight into what the Bible really says about insipid Christianity. It is also my hope that you will want to change. You can, you know!

What You Decide Affects Your Relationship with God

The third implication one can draw from the principle of control is this: What you decide will determine the reality and the peace of God in your life. Paul, after telling his friends in Philippi to think about certain things because it could make a difference, makes a very interesting statement:

> The things which you learned and received and heard and saw in me, these do, and the God of peace will be with you. (Philippians 4:9)

I don't know about you, but there is a strange paradox I have discovered in my life. When I am too frightened to make waves for Christ, when I have chosen to go over in a corner to avoid conflict and problems, when I have chosen to take the easy way out and when I have chosen to allow my faith to be insipid, I find that my anxiety level rises. In fact, that which I think will lessen my worry and anxiety does just the opposite. However, I have found that, when I stand, God stands with me.

In Acts 5, you will remember, the apostles are in prison for standing for Christ, but, "at night an angel of the Lord opened the prison doors and brought them out" (Acts 5:19).

When was the last time you saw an angel? Probably it's been a long time, if ever. Let me ask you another question: When was the last time you were in prison? If we went to prison more, we would see more angels.

The point is this: Our efforts to obtain peace by quietly slinking off into a corner, trying to stay out of the way and keeping our mouths shut, are fruitless. In fact, the best way to find peace is to stand boldly for Christ because, if you stand, He will stand with you. Now it is time to get down to business—the business of shattering the stereotype and saying "no" to manipulation.

Knowledge and principles, though, are not enough. God has to grant us His grace to change. Our prayer ought to be the prayer of the sea captain in the middle of a hurricane: "O God, help us and come Yourself because this ain't no time for boys."

2

A Powerful Priesthood

The Uniqueness of Christian Boldness

One of the good things about working on a book is that, in the process, you find yourself changing. If it is a good book and faithful to the Scriptures, the change is usually for the better. This book, because of its nature, is written with an even higher expectation of change . . . not only for me, but for you as well.

There are some very real dangers in change, however, especially when that change is in the direction of boldness and freedom. There is great risk involved—of rejection, criticism and fear on the part of others. (We'll get to that later!) But, aside from that risk, there is the danger of becoming something God never intended.

We have all heard the platitudes of wisdom such as, "A rose by any other name" and "If it walks like a duck, looks like a duck and quacks like a duck, it must be a duck." Most of the time, when you look at a rose, you can call it anything you like, but it is still a rose. And when you come across anything that looks, walks and quacks like a duck, it usually is a duck. But not always. Let's talk about exceptions.

Counterfeit Freedom and Joy

Someone has said that Satan will use 99 percent of the truth to float one lie. That is correct and, because it is, it is terribly important that we, as Christians, be careful as to how we assess new religions, new believers, new doctrines and new books—even this one.

I remember the day that I found myself free. I didn't have to please everybody; I didn't have to be Billy Graham; I didn't have to be guilty all the time; I didn't have to smile at everybody; I didn't have to come up to everybody's expectations of me; I didn't have to be kind, nice and sweet. I felt as if the world had been lifted off my shoulders. I could cry out with the slave after emancipation: "I'm free! I'm free! Praise God Almighty, I'm free at last!"

Now, the problem with the freedom and the joy I feel is that there are many others who express the same freedom and joy— and they are not Christians. I have heard graduates of EST, adherents to the principles of Scientology and Transcendental Meditation and people who have had a "numinous" encounter with God, all express a similar experience. That used to bother me a great deal. Because they talked about freedom and joy, did it mean they had the same source? Was God the center of a spoked wheel, and, like the spokes, were there many different ways to Him? Did we all, at the center of things, really believe the same thing? Did it matter what one believed as long as one was sincere about it?

Professor William Kilpatrick, in his very good book written a number of years ago, *Psychological Seduction*, speaks about the necessity of having something better to offer others than an experience. He says:

> I sometimes ask my students, many of whom look forward to careers in the helping professions, what they will have to offer— say, to the alcoholic—that's better than "god in a bottle." Their answers tend to be framed along psychological lines: "adjustment to society," "coping," "a better self-concept," and so forth. Those responses, it seems to me, miss the point. If you can have god in a bottle, and temporarily be a god yourself, why would you settle for such paltry things as adjustment or coping? Once you have tasted transcendence, even the spurious kind, it is no easy matter to come back to earth.[4]

The question is this: What is the difference between my experience and the experience of others if we describe the experience in the same way? If someone can find freedom and joy in a bottle, what is the difference between my freedom and joy and his? The difference is in the source of the experience and in the truth that comes from it. Most believers don't realize there is a counterfeit to almost everything God does in the believer's life. A counterfeit is not the real thing, but it is close enough to be passed off to the unwary as real. That is why one must be very careful to judge "experience" on the basis of the truth of Scripture, not on the existence of experience itself.

> Now the Spirit expressly says that in latter times some will depart from the faith, giving heed to deceiving spirits and doctrines of demons. (1 Timothy 4:1)

This point is also clearly made in 1 John 4:1–3:

> Beloved, do not believe every spirit, but test the spirits, whether they are of God; because many false prophets have gone out into the world. By this you know the Spirit of God: Every spirit that confesses that Jesus Christ has come in the flesh is of God, and every spirit that does not confess that Jesus Christ has come in the flesh is not of God. And this is the spirit of the Antichrist, which you have heard was coming, and is now already in the world.

The reason I am saying all this is to attach a very important warning to everything that is said in this book: All boldness is not Christian boldness. Or to put it another way: Just because you are bold does not mean that you are Christian. It may simply be that you have a "mean streak."

It is not my desire to see Christians becoming narrow, negative and abrasive. I do think the boldness that comes from Christ may make you more narrow than you are now; it may enable you to say "no" more often; it may make you more confrontational than you are now. But it is terribly important that you understand the difference between what comes from God and what is simply a selfish need to control and intimidate others.

So, I want to show you the difference between Christian boldness and the boldness that comes from the teachings of, say, a Wayne Dyer or a Hobart Mowrer. There will be certain parallels, of course, but there are significant differences. If it looks, walks and quacks like a duck—it just may not be a duck.

The Uniqueness of Christian Boldness

What then is the difference between Christian boldness and "pulling your own strings," "looking out for number one," or "winning through intimidation"? In other words: What makes Christian boldness different from pagan boldness?

A key verse for this discussion is found in Paul's second letter to his young friend, Timothy. Paul said:

For God has not given us a spirit of fear, but of power and of love and of a sound mind. (2 Timothy 1:7)

From the Scripture, there are four distinguishing marks of Christian boldness. Let's check them out.

Christian Boldness Is Courageous

First, Christian boldness is courageous (i.e., not "a spirit of fear"). Courage is not acting boldly without fear; it is, rather, acting in spite of fear. When Paul said that God hadn't given the Christian a spirit of fear, he didn't mean there is no more fear. He meant, rather, that the debilitating fear which often paralyzes the Christian is not sold in the store of God.

Anyone who lives in our kind of world without fear is a fool. In Mark Twain's cynical, small novel, *The Mysterious Stranger*, the mysterious stranger tells a little boy that a certain man who is anxiety-ridden will live his entire life in happiness. Then the man goes insane. The little boy is angry and bitter because he feels betrayed. But Satan (the mysterious stranger) says this:

> What an ass you are! Are you so unobservant as not to have found out that sanity and happiness are an impossible combination? No sane man can be happy, for to him life is real, and he sees what a fearful thing it is. Only the mad can be happy, and not many of those. The few that imagine themselves kings or gods are happy, the rest are no happier than the sane . . . I have taken from this man that trumpery thing which the race regards as a Mind; I have replaced his tin life with a silver-gilt fiction; you see the result— and you criticize! I said I would make him permanently happy, and I have done it. I have made him happy by the only means possible to his race—and you are not satisfied![5]

Too many Christians walk around with the feeling that to be human is a sin. So, we think Christians don't get depressed or angry or afraid. That isn't what Paul said, though. He said that real Christian boldness is courage that comes in the face of real fear. We live in a fallen world where the dangers are very real. What Christ does with the Christian is to give him or her a spirit of courage.

I remember a board meeting I once attended when the whole board was negative on a position about which I was positive. I was the newest member of the board; and, to be perfectly honest, I was intimidated by the others (well-known Christian business-men and national Christian leaders) and had determined, at least in the beginning, to keep my mouth shut. (The principle: Better to be thought a fool than to open one's mouth and remove all doubt!) But I felt so strongly on this particular issue that I felt I ought to say something. So I did.

The problem was once I started . . . I couldn't stop. Something inside was saying to me, "Shut up, you fool." But I still kept talking. Not only was I talking, but I was talking in unbelievably strong terms. When it was over, I felt like going somewhere and hiding. The motion was tabled, and you could have heard a pin drop. It was one of those embarrassing situations similar to the reaction of an audience to a soloist who can't sing, but is doing his or her best.

And then, at the next board meeting, I found that the whole board had changed its mind and reversed itself. The board voted unanimously in favor of my position. Where in the world did I get the courage? I'll tell you where. I got it from God.

Over and over again in church history, we see ordinary men and women God set on fire. They were as much surprised as anyone else. For instance, Thomas Cranmer was a weak and compromising man. In the sixteenth century, he sided with Henry VIII in the king's efforts to be rid of his wife. While holding some Protestant doctrines, his real allegiance was to the king because he had seen what could happen if one were too strong in one's theological views. He had watched Nicholas Ridley and Hugh Latimer die at the stake, and he knew the same thing could happen to him.

With the fear that can only come when you have faced a horrible reality, in writing, he renounced his former views. Then, as the time of his own death by fire approached, something happened to this weak man. Cranmer stood before the crowd who had gathered to see his execution and cried, "And now I come to the great thing which so much troubleth my conscience, more than any thing that ever I did or said in my whole life, and that is the scattering abroad of writing contrary to the truth [referring to his written renunciation]." Cranmer then renounced his turning from the truth and said, "And forasmuch as my hand hath offended, writing contrary to my heart, therefore this my hand shall first be punished, for when I come to the fire, it shall first be burned."[6]

When Cranmer was brought before the stake, he placed his hand, the offending hand with which he had written his renunciation of the truth, in the fire and watched his hand burn before he stepped into the flames himself. Where in the world did this man get that kind of courage? How hard did he have to work to obtain it? He didn't. It was a gift from the Father, who creates bold Christians.

Christian Boldness Is Powerful

Second, Paul said that Christian boldness as opposed to pagan boldness is not only courageous, it is also powerful. What was it in Queen Mary, one of the most powerful monarchs on the face of the earth, that caused her to cringe before John Knox? Knox was only a little man with a very weak and frail body.

Mary, in her frustration with Knox, is said to have cried out to him: "I have borne with you in all your rigorous manner of speaking, both against myself and against my uncles; yea, I have sought your favor by all possible means; I have offered unto you presents and audience whence wherever it pleased you to admonish me, and yet I can not be quit of you. I vow to God I shall be once revenged."

Knox replied, "Madam, I am not master of myself, but must obey Him who commands me to speak plain, and to flatter no flesh upon the face of the earth."[7]

Why did Mary fear the prayers of John Knox more than an army of ten-thousand men? Thomas McCrie said, "I know not if ever so much piety and genius were lodged in such a frail and weak body. Certain I am that it will be difficult to find one in whom the gifts of the Holy Spirit shone so bright to the comfort of the church in Scotland."[8]

There is supernatural power in the boldness of the Christian. That power is not always successful, but it is always effective. God takes common men and women and sends them out with a powerful message anointed by a powerful God. The Father sets men and women on fire.

Christian boldness is an awesome thing to watch. I have seen grown men weep before it; I have seen drug addicts turn from their drugs and alcoholics turn from their bottles because of it; I have seen soldiers cringe in its light; I have seen angry, hostile, abrasive people back away from their plans in the face of it; I have seen sinners repent and saints grow as they are prodded by it. There is something supernaturally powerful about Christian boldness. The problem is that few people have seen that power simply because not many Christians are willing to exercise it.

During the French Revolution, a speaker in the Legislative Assembly asked, "Why do not our great men, our priests and philosophers, move and save the people?"

A woman in the audience shouted back, "Because they are cast in bronze."

That is the problem. All the boldness in the world is nothing but empty wind. It rails, rants and demands its rights. Nothing ever changes, though, until the terrible people of God stand up. That is when history is changed, lives are changed and circumstances are changed. The change doesn't come because of the Christian's boldness, but because of God's application of power to the Christian's boldness. That power is one of the ways you can tell the difference between Christian and pagan boldness.

Christian Boldness Is Loving

Third, Paul said that Christian boldness is not only courageous and powerful, it is also loving.

As surprising as it may sound, real love is as hard as nails. It is love that refuses to let go until the lover is loved and knows it. A friend of mine said to me once, "Steve, you are a very hard person to love; but, before God, I am determined to love you and I will."

A number of years ago, Jerry Falwell was invited by Mark Tanenbaum, International Interreligious Affairs Director for the American Jewish Committee, to address a national gathering of conservative Jewish rabbis at a large hotel on Miami Beach. My friend, Bill Gralnick, who works with the AJC, was able to obtain a hard-to-come-by ticket for me. It was an interesting meeting.

Jerry Falwell, who certainly does not represent the views of most rabbis in this country, had come into what appeared to be very hostile territory. Mark Tanenbaum, who has done so much to further understanding between Evangelicals and Jews, was not a popular man that evening. As I sat in the audience, trying to look as Jewish as possible, I heard comments of anger expressed about

Dr. Tanenbaum for having invited this right-wing, Fundamentalist preacher.

It was interesting to watch the body language of the rabbis attending that meeting. The body language reflected a high degree of hostility—arms crossed in anger, raised eyebrows and angry expressions. But, as Falwell began to speak, I noticed a gradual change taking place in the audience. The arms unfolded, the frowns turned to smiles and the angry expressions turned into expressions of interest. Soon the rabbis were leaning forward to listen to what Falwell was saying. And, the more he talked, the more it became apparent that he was winning a hearing. He did not convert any of the rabbis, of course. He didn't try. But his love for them and what they stood for was so apparent that they were willing to listen. His speech was interrupted several times by applause.

During the question and answer session following his speech, Falwell was asked, "What do you want from us?"

Falwell's answer was astounding. He said. "I don't want anything from you. I have everything I need and want. I have come here to tell you that I am going to be your friend, and even if you don't want me to be your friend, I'm still going to be your friend. I have come here to tell you that I love you, and even if you don't want me to love you, I am still going to love you. That is the only reason I came."

Jerry Falwell is not a very popular figure in some circles; but that night I saw a demonstration I won't soon forget of Christian boldness characterized by love. My brother's bold love was an inspiration.

A Christian is bold, but if that boldness is not also characterized by love, the whole point of the boldness is lost. Anybody can be bold . . . but to be lovingly bold is no small thing. Love remembers the other person. Love looks out for the interests of others. Love sometimes is harsh, strong and even angry. But it is never destructive.

I once asked my friend, Fred Smith, one of the wisest Christians I know, the difference between motivation and manipulation. They often appear to be the same thing. Fred said that, while manipulation is for the benefit of the one doing the manipulating, motivation is for the benefit of the motivator *and* the one being motivated. I like that, because it is similar to Christian boldness. Christians don't "win through intimidation." They don't have to! Christian boldness is a boldness that never forgets the other person. You file that kind of boldness under love.

Christian Boldness Has a "Sound Mind"

And then finally, Paul said that Christian boldness, as opposed to pagan boldness, is characterized by a "sound mind." The Greek word Paul uses here for "sound mind" is not an easy word to translate into English. It doesn't mean exactly (as some translations have it) self-control; but rather, discipline or perhaps the ability to generate discipline in oneself and in others. It is the ability to control oneself in the face of pressure situations.

That is one of the great differences between Christian boldness and pagan boldness. Pagan boldness is often a simple, visceral reaction to unpleasant circumstances. ("You turkey! Look what you did to my car. If you would watch where you're going, you idiot, it wouldn't happen.") Christian boldness, on the other hand, is planned, directed and controlled. It is not power without pressure, but power under pressure.

A number of years ago, a good friend of mine by the name of Blair Richardson went Home to be with the Lord. That isn't the sad part. The sad part is that he was a young man who had a wonderful wife and a baby on the way.

As a prize fighter, Blair found Christ through the ministry of my friend, John DeBrine. He held a number of prize-fighting titles and was on his way up. Right after he found Christ, John often asked Blair to give his testimony. I used to wonder why John did that; because, to be perfectly honest with you, Blair simply couldn't talk. I thought someone ought to give Blair speech lessons!

Anyway, Blair would sometimes set up a fighting ring down in the slums of Boston to demonstrate his gift of prize fighting. When he got a crowd of young people together, he would tell them about

Jesus. By the time Blair died, he had become a very fine communicator with his voice as well as his fists. He was even teaching speech at one of the colleges in Boston. Blair was used all over the country because he had a tremendous gift with young people.

The church near Boston where I was then the pastor had scheduled Blair to speak to the youth. I called him a few weeks before the meeting to confirm that he was coming. I asked him how he was doing, and he said he was fine, but that he had a little headache.

"Don't worry, Steve," he said, "I'm going to be there, and we are going to see God do a great thing." That night, however, Blair was rushed to the hospital and, before the dawn, was dead from a brain tumor.

John DeBrine talked to Blair's wife, Beverly, shortly after Blair's death. He told her, "Beverly, up to this point, when you have talked about your relationship to Christ, people have listened, but most people have said, 'Sure, she's a Christian. She has everything going for her. A husband who looks like a Greek god, a baby on the way, a wonderful life. If I had all that, I would be a Christian too.' But, Beverly, those same people are still watching, and they want to know if your faith works in the hard places. They will hear what you say now a lot more than they heard before, so be careful."

Of course, our young people were devastated that Blair had died, but we decided to have the youth banquet anyway. And, while Beverly Richardson couldn't come, she did write a letter to be read at the banquet. Let me quote from that letter:

Dear Young People,

Since I am unable to be with you at your banquet, I wanted to send along greetings to you by letter.

As you can well imagine these are difficult days, but I want you to know that my Savior, Jesus Christ, knows and understands. He has surrounded me with His love and given real peace in my heart.

The wonderful thing about the sorrow I feel over my personal loss of Blair is that it is a sorrow with hope! Blair is with our Lord

in heaven and far happier now than even when we were together—
and we were very happy.

Why do I know where Blair is right now? Is it because Blair was
a good man? No. Is it because he tried to help young people? No.
Well, then is it because he always went to church? No. Blair is in
heaven today because he was a sinner saved by what Jesus Christ
did for him on Calvary's cross. When Blair was twenty-one, he came
humbly to the Savior and confessed that he indeed was a sinner
and asked Jesus to come with forgiveness and live through his life.
On March 5th Blair saw the Lord face to face.

Young people, I know that Blair certainly did not expect to leave
us that day, but he was ready. He had no opportunity for a last
minute decision for Christ.

Tonight I would ask those of you who have not accepted Jesus
Christ to take a good look at your life. What is it that would hold
you back? The things of this world satisfy for only a brief time, but
our Savior gives true meaning to life here on earth and then eter-
nal life with Him. Is anything here worth keeping us from that?

For those of us who are Christians, I would ask that we really
recommit our lives to the Lord so that He can really use us. There
are so many who do not know Christ. Won't you let Him use you
to lead others to Him in the days ahead?

You will be in my thoughts and prayers tonight. Let this be the
most important night of your lives!

With Love in Christ,
Beverly Richardson

That letter is the best definition I know of for what Paul said
characterizes Christian boldness. I can see someone writing a letter like that a couple of years after the death of one they loved. But
to write that kind of letter less than two weeks after her husband
had died is nothing less than a demonstration of self-control and
a sound mind.

Christian boldness is sometimes similar to pagan boldness, but
pagan boldness is a counterfeit. Frank Sinatra sang, "I did it my
way." Christians must sing, "I did it the Father's way." Christian
boldness and freedom are always from the Father and for the
Father . . . and that makes all the difference in the world.

3

A Philosophy
Biblical Boldness

As we saw in the previous chapter, Christian boldness is unique.
Now, let's get down to the specifics. I have heard more times than
I care to remember that Christians are called to be doormats. We
are not to be bold or assertive. Well, that smells like smoke and
comes from the pit of hell! In this chapter, I want to show you how
to say "no" and yet still be a Christian.

The key is:

> But let your "Yes" be "Yes," and your "No," "No." For whatever is
> more than these is from the evil one. (Matthew 5:37)

Do you remember Shadrach, Meshach and Abed-Nego? Their
story begins in Daniel 3:1–7:

> Nebuchadnezzar the king made an image of gold, whose height
> was sixty cubits and its width six cubits. He set it up in the plain
> of Dura, in the province of Babylon. And King Nebuchadnezzar
> sent word to gather together the satraps, the administrators, the
> governors, the counselors, the treasurers, the judges, the magis-
> trates, and all the officials of the provinces, to come to the dedica-
> tion of the image which King Nebuchadnezzar had set up. So the
> satraps, the administrators, the governors, the counselors, the trea-
> surers, the judges, the magistrates, and all the officials of the
> provinces gathered together for the dedication of the image that
> King Nebuchadnezzar had set up; and they stood before the image
> that Nebuchadnezzar had set up. Then a herald cried aloud: "To

you it is commanded, O peoples, nations, and languages, that at the time you hear the sound of the horn, flute, harp, lyre, and psaltery, in symphony with all kinds of music, you shall fall down and worship the gold image that King Nebuchadnezzar has set up; and whoever does not fall down and worship shall be cast immediately into the midst of a burning fiery furnace." So at that time, when all the people heard the sound of the horn, flute, harp, and lyre, in symphony with all kinds of music, all the people, nations, and languages fell down and worshiped the gold image which King Nebuchadnezzar had set up.

Shadrach, Meshach and Abed-Nego absolutely refused to join in the worship of the gold image. The king told them that, if they continued to refuse, they would face the fire, to which they replied:

"If that is the case, our God whom we serve is able to deliver us from the burning fiery furnace, and He will deliver us from your hand, O king. But if not, let it be known to you, O king, that we do not serve your gods, nor will we worship the gold image which you have set up." (3:17–18)

Later on in the book of Daniel, there was another king by the name of Darius and Daniel was highly favored by him. As a result, the other leaders were jealous, so they talked King Darius into making a royal statue of himself. Not only that, they got the king to decree that, for thirty days, no one in the kingdom could worship any other god but the statue of the king. During the dedicatory period, the penalty for someone failing to obey that decree was for the person to be thrown to the lions.

What did Daniel do?

Now when Daniel knew that the writing was signed, he went home. And in his upper room, with his windows open toward Jerusalem, he knelt down on his knees three times that day, and prayed and gave thanks before his God, as was his custom since early days. (6:10)

Those four members of our family were bold believers! Don't forget about Shadrach, Meshach, Abed-Nego and Daniel. They will serve as our models as we go through assertiveness training for Christians.

Do you know what I see more than anything else in the lives of Christians? As I pointed out before, they are tired, just plain tired. Maybe you are tired for the same reasons.

- Are you tired of saying "yes" when you really want to say "no"?
- Are you tired of being a doormat?
- Are you tired of listening to the pontification of sour saints, knowing all along that what they're saying is nonsense? (And you still have to smile!)
- Are you tired of being manipulated?
- Are you tired of bearing responsibility for every problem suffered by mankind?
- Are you tired of feeling guilty when you haven't done anything wrong?
- Are you tired of going along with Christians for harmony's sake?
- Are you tired of being like everybody else?
- Are you tired of being afraid to ask questions?
- Are you afraid of doing anything improper?
- Are you sick and tired of being a Christian wimp?

If you can identify, this is for you . . . I'm going to teach you how to offend some people!

My friend, Norm Evans, played football in college, later for the Miami Dolphins and then, for the Seattle Seahawks. Evans said that, one time, there was a freshman lineman with a professional football team who ran over to the coach during a time out and complained, "The opposing lineman keeps pulling my helmet down over my eyes. What should I do?"

The coach smiled and said, "Don't let him. Just don't let him."

I believe that coach should have given the football player some practical help. That is what this chapter is designed to do—to give you some practical help. I'm going to tell you, "Don't let him"; but, not only that, I'm going to show you how. So, let's get to it.

A number of years ago, I was involved in a gathering of Christians in Washington, D.C. It was an exciting time as hundreds of thousands of Christians gathered just to make a positive witness for Christ in the nation's capital. At a luncheon preceding the main gathering, to be honest with you, we were frightened about what was going to happen during the mass demonstration. We were afraid that some neurotic Christians might say something they shouldn't say. We were afraid that some pagans would jump on us. We were afraid that the press would misinterpret what was going on. We were afraid that, in the enthusiasm of the moment, there would be violence. We were afraid of a lot of things.

At that luncheon, a black bishop rose from his chair and asked for the attention of the group. He said, "Brothers and sisters, I have a message from the Lord." The room suddenly became quiet as he continued, "The Lord says that if you Christians ever get over your fear, you are going to be dangerous."

This chapter is about Christians getting over their fear. And the place to begin is with the biblical doctrine of boldness. The doctrine of boldness has four elements.

A Christian's Model

First, a Christian philosophy of boldness should include a Christian's model.

> Let this mind be in you which was also in Christ Jesus, who, being in the form of God, did not consider it robbery to be equal with

God, but made Himself of no reputation, taking the form of a bond-servant, and coming in the likeness of men. (Philippians 2:5–7)

My friend, Dave O'Dowd, once was a guest on a talk show in Miami, debating another person on capital punishment. Dave took the side for capital punishment; the other person took the side against it. Dave is an ordained pastor and seminary professor and, for that reason, the man with whom my friend debated thought that he had finally put Dave into a corner, when he said, "Dr. O'Dowd, can you imagine Jesus pulling the lever on an electric chair?"

Dave was quiet for a moment. Then, he smiled and answered, "As I read my Bible, He is going to do a whole lot worse than that!"

You see, the problem with most pagans is that they only think of gentle Jesus, meek and mild. Jesus is that, but He is a lot more. Look at John 2:13–25:

Now the Passover of the Jews was at hand, and Jesus went up to Jerusalem. And He found in the temple those who sold oxen and sheep and doves, and the moneychangers doing business. When He had made a whip of cords, He drove them all out of the temple, with the sheep and the oxen, and poured out the changers' money and overturned the tables. And He said to those who sold doves, "Take these things away! Do not make My Father's house a house of merchandise!" Then His disciples remembered that it was written, "Zeal for Your house has eaten Me up." So the Jews answered and said to Him, "What sign do You show to us, since you do these things?" Jesus answered and said to them, "Destroy this temple, and in three days I will raise it up." Then the Jews said, "It has taken forty-six years to build this temple, and will You raise it up in three days?" But He was speaking of the temple of His body. Therefore, when He had risen from the dead, His disciples remembered that He had said this to them; and they believed the Scripture and the word which Jesus had said. Now when He was in Jerusalem at the Passover, during the feast, many believed in His name when they saw the signs which He did. But Jesus did not commit Himself to them, because He knew all men, and had no need that anyone should testify of man, for He knew what was in man.

I saw a bumper sticker once that read, "Jesus is coming back and boy, is He ticked!" There is something to that. If Jesus can express His anger, we can too. However, there is a five-way test to the anger Jesus expressed. When we're angry, we need to put our anger through the same test.

Jesus' Anger Was Restrained

First, Jesus' anger was restrained. When I was a pastor, a friend of mine brought her psychiatrist brother to a worship service. After the sermon, as they were leaving, my friend asked her brother what he thought about me. He said, "I have never seen anyone living so close to the edge of hostility."

Let me tell you something by way of confession. I get angry easily. Jesus got angry too, but He was not an angry man. Can you be described as an angry man or woman? In other words: *Is your life characterized by anger?*

When I was a student at Boston University, my teachers wanted to believe that, if there was ever another incarnation, Jesus, of course, would be a liberal, Socialist member of the Greenpeace organization. There are those who think that, if Jesus came back, He would be a Republican or a feminist. That simply won't wash because Jesus refuses to fit into our little molds.

It is very hard to think of Jesus as an angry man. While I find that I have no trouble in thinking of Jesus as strong, loving, compassionate and wise, I have great difficulty in thinking of Him as angry.

Jesus said, "Come to Me, all you who labor and are heavy laden, and I will give you rest. Take My yoke upon you and learn from Me, for I am gentle and lowly in heart, and you will find rest for your souls" (Matthew 11:28–29).

While Jesus got angry, His anger was restrained. He had plenty about which to be angry, though. There was the frustration of not being understood. There was the dullness of His disciples. When Jesus was in trouble, all His disciples fled and one of His closest followers denied Him. Jesus came to serve, and He found His followers arguing about who would be the greatest in the kingdom. While He encountered indifference, rebellion and unbelief—Jesus can't be thought of as an angry man.

If I'm going to use Jesus as my model, I will sometimes get angry; but if my friends think of me as an angry person, or if I'm angry most of the time, then I have missed it.

When you are angry, you need to ask yourself: *Is my anger restrained?*

Jesus' Anger Was Selfless

Second, Jesus' anger was selfless. In other words, Jesus wasn't angry because someone stepped on His toe. Jesus wasn't angry because He didn't get what was coming to Him. Jesus wasn't angry because someone crossed him or because someone had not been nice to Him. Jesus wasn't angry because someone failed to speak to Him.

Jesus was angry because others had been hurt. He was concerned for the poor and the oppressed. While we can't entirely meet this measurement, our anger should be as much as possible over other people's hurt . . . not so much over our own hurt.

Jesus' anger was never ego-centered and, the problem is, ours almost always is. If I could ever work up my anger over someone else's hurt or rejection, I would be able to be more like Jesus.

When the prophets cried out against injustice, they did it for two reasons. First, God told them to speak; and second, they were angry about a situation that hurt people. That should be our aim.

I am not saying that there is no legitimate anger when one is personally involved. However, I am saying that, if most of our anger is because we have been hurt, crossed or ignored, it is not the kind of anger Jesus expressed. Jesus ought to have been angry at His betrayal; He ought to have been angry at His trial; He ought to have been angry while He was hanging on the cross. And, yet, Jesus was not angry in those places—only hurt. That says a lot about His concern. The concern of Jesus was for others, and His anger reflected that concern.

When the missionary, James Calvert, went out to Fiji in 1838, the captain of the ship on which he sailed told Calvert that he was going to a land of cannibals.

The captain tried to dissuade Calvert from going, saying, "You are risking your life and all those with you if you go among such savages. You will all die!"

Calvert replied, "We died before we came here."

The Christian goes through a process of dying, of being crucified with Christ. In so far as that process is progressing, we will be angry less about what others do to us and more about what is done to others.

When you are angry, you need to ask yourself: *Is my anger selfless?*

Jesus' Anger Was Righteous

Third, Jesus' anger was not only restrained and selfless; it was also righteous. The anger of Jesus can be characterized as righteous indignation. He was angry simply because a just God had been offended.

Not too long ago, I spoke at a Christian college. The chaplain asked me if it would be okay for him to set up some counseling appointments with me for some of the students. I agreed, and the college set me up in a small office with some secretarial help to keep the appointments in order.

I sat down behind the desk, expecting to encounter the common problems of students—questions about sexuality, suicide and relationships.

I was surprised, however, when instead, student after student told me how one professor on campus had weakened and sometimes destroyed their faith.

The more I listened, the angrier I became. Fuming, by the end of the day, I was ready to go after this particular professor. Then, I realized the damage I could cause if I didn't control and direct my anger.

I asked God to forgive me for my anger and, in my spirit, I heard Him say, "Son, there is nothing to forgive. I am more angry than you are. Control it . . . but use it." I did, and the professor is no longer teaching at that college.

Dr. Donald Grey Barnhouse, a former pastor of Tenth Presbyterian Church in Philadelphia, had a question and answer session on most Wednesday evenings. One evening, a woman in the front row raised her hand and said, "Dr. Barnhouse, I attend a church where the pastor doesn't believe in the Virgin Birth, the Resurrection or the Bible. What should I do?"

Those who were there said that Dr. Barnhouse took off his glasses, smiled and, in total seriousness, said, "Madam, you should pray that he die."

Then, Dr. Barnhouse put his glasses back on and went to the next question. Improper anger? No, I don't think so. It was righteous indignation. I think Barnhouse expressed God's anger . . . and sometimes God gets very angry! I have often prayed, "Father, teach me to weep where you weep, to love what you love, and to be angry where you are angry."

Anger can be right when it reflects God's anger. Are you angry about drugs, abortion and heresy? You do well.

When you are angry, you need to ask yourself: *Is my anger righteous?*

Jesus' Anger Was Controlled

Fourth, Jesus' anger was controlled.

Do you remember when Barry Goldwater ran for President in 1964? (I voted for him because I was a student at Boston University and got tired of them making fun of him!) At any rate, Barry Goldwater is a man of great integrity. He would come to Florida and speak against the excesses of Social Security. Not only that, Goldwater would go to Tennessee and speak against the Tennessee Valley Authority. Needless to say, he wasn't the kind of politician who said only what people wanted!

I once heard former Senator Walter Judd tell about the time he went to Goldwater and said, "Barry, you have got to learn that sometimes it is best to be quiet. Every time you pass a bull in a field, you don't have to wave a red flag in his face."

Jesus would have agreed with Judd's advice. Jesus' anger was controlled. Before He went to the temple, Jesus took the time to braid the strands of a whip. There were also plenty of violations of God's law at which Jesus could have expressed anger, but didn't. Jesus picked His time and His place.

I remember when I served as a pastor of a little church on Cape Cod. All winter, we struggled to keep that church together. The church sat only a small number of people; we had only a few each Sunday morning. Then Easter came. I was back in my study, watching the ushers bring the chairs out when I realized that the church was packed. All the pagans had come to show off their Easter finery. Do you know what that did to me? It really ticked me off! It was my first Easter as a pastor and I was so mad I could spit.

All I could do was pace back and forth in my study, thinking about how I was going to get those turkeys! The janitor at the church came into my study and said, "Sit down, pastor." Then he said, "Don't blow it. You only get one shot and it is today."

His words were like cold water. I didn't quit being angry, but I stopped and thought about it. Then, I used my anger to speak clearly and strongly about God's action in raising Jesus from the dead. There was power in that sermon because it was the power of controlled anger.

When Jesus got angry, He took the time to braid a whip. If we would take the time to braid our whips, we would be more effective in our anger.

Socrates had a good point when he said, "Getting angry is not the issue. It is when, where and how you get angry."

When you are angry, you need to ask yourself: *Is my anger controlled?*

Jesus' Anger Was Effective

Jesus' anger was not only restrained, selfless, righteous and controlled. It was, fifthly and finally, effective. The anger of Jesus accomplished something. In this particular incident in John, Christ taught on the resurrection. Jesus made a point and people believed in Him. Note that the religious leaders did not question the propriety of Jesus' actions. Rather, they asked Him if He had a sign to show that He had the authority to do what He did. It was that question which opened the door for a witness from Jesus that caused belief.

One time, the former President of Czechoslovakia visited the Paris office of a news service. One of the correspondents noted that the president never became angry. The newsman commented on it and asked the reason.

The president replied, "I am a short man, and short men must never become angry. When a big man becomes enraged, it seems impressive; but, when a little man gets angry and starts sputtering and fuming, he just looks silly." Jesus was a very big man. His anger was impressive.

We must be careful, however, because we are very little. We ought to be angry, but we must be careful lest we appear only silly.

I don't even remember the issue, but one time I got so angry with an officer in the church that I locked my study door so that he couldn't get out while I gave him a "piece of my mind." (I know, I was awfully young then and it was really stupid.) Later on, though, I went and asked for the officer's forgiveness. We are still friends, but do you know what that accomplished? Nothing. Absolutely nothing. He never came back to the church. The English say, "Don't get mad, get back." That is not Christian, but it makes a good point.

When you are angry, you need to ask yourself, finally: *Is my anger effective?*

A Creator's Responsibility

Now, to the second point in our philosophy of Christian boldness: A Christian philosophy of boldness should not only include a Christian's model, it should also include a Creator's responsibility. A Christian philosophy of boldness should let the Creator assume the responsibility that is His.

What is the Creator's responsibility?

> For of Him and through Him and to Him are all things, to whom be glory forever. Amen. (Romans 11:36)

> And my God shall supply all your need according to His riches in glory by Christ Jesus. (Philippians 4:19)

> Now may the God of peace Himself sanctify you completely; and may your whole spirit, soul, and body be preserved blameless at the coming of our Lord Jesus Christ. (1 Thessalonians 5:23)

We have touched on this before, but it won't hurt to hear it again: Often, we don't say "no" simply because we believe that we are personally responsible for all the problems in the world.

Let me illustrate from Thomas Kelly's book once again. He puts it well:

> But it is a particularization of my responsibility in a world too vast and a lifetime too short for me to carry all responsibilities. My cosmic love, or the Divine Lover loving within me, cannot accomplish its full intent, which is universal saviorhood, within the limits of three score years and ten. But the Loving Presence does not burden us equally with all things, but considerately puts upon each of us just a few central tasks, as emphatic responsibilities. For each of us these special undertakings are our share in the joyous burdens of love.
>
> Thus the state of having a concern has a foreground and a background. In the foreground is the special task, uniquely illuminated, toward which we feel a special yearning and care . . . But in the background is a second level, or layer, of universal concern for all

the multitude of good things that need doing. Toward them all we feel kindly, but we are dismissed from active service in most of them. And we have an easy mind in the presence of desperately real needs which are not our direct responsibility. We cannot die on every cross, nor are we expected to.[9]

Let me give you some lies:

"It will hurt my witness if I don't do everything that is expected."
"If people don't like me, they won't like God."
"God needs help in running His universe."

Those are all lies. Everything is God's responsibility. Only what He has given you is yours . . . and, even then, it is ultimately His. So, when somebody manipulates you with guilt to get you to do something that God has not called you to do, simply say, "No." A philosophy of Christian boldness should include a Creator's responsibility.

A Believer's Rights

Third, a Christian philosophy of boldness should include a believer's rights. Let me show you what the Bible teaches.

But as many as received Him, to them He gave the right to become children of God, even to those who believe in His name. (John 1:12)

Paul said in 1 Corinthians 9:1–6:

Am I not an apostle? Am I not free? Have I not seen Jesus Christ our Lord? Are you not my work in the Lord? If I am not an apostle to others, yet doubtless I am to you. For you are the seal of my apostleship in the Lord. My defense to those who examine me is this: Do we have no right to eat and drink? Do we have no right to take along a believing wife, as do also the other apostles, the brothers of the Lord, and Cephas? Or is it only Barnabas and I who have no right to refrain from working?

Old Testament law, contrary to what you may believe, is not just a list of the obligations of God's people. It is also a list of the rights of God's people. Now, a Christian may or may not choose to turn over his or her rights; but, for God's sake, don't tell me that a Christian has no rights. It is simply not true. There are eight rights which are very, very important. Let's check them out.

You Have the Right to Be Human

First, you have the right to be human.

> But when He saw the multitudes, He was moved with compassion for them, because they were weary and scattered. (Matthew 9:36)

> For I determined not to know anything among you except Jesus Christ and Him crucified. I was with you in weakness, in fear, and in much trembling. And my speech and my preaching were not with persuasive words of human wisdom, but in demonstration of the Spirit and of power, that your faith should not be in the wisdom of men but in the power of God. (1 Corinthians 2:2–5)

> For He knows our frame; He remembers that we are dust. (Psalm 103:14)

Do you know what it means to be human? It means that sometimes you will be angry and withdrawn. Sometimes you will be tired. Sometimes you will just want to go away and cry. Sometimes you will want to junk the whole thing and walk away.

I said once to a depressed man with a number of problems, "Good Lord, man, of course you are depressed! If you weren't, you wouldn't be normal." He smiled, relieved. Why? Because I gave him the right to be human. The fact is, Christians bleed. Christians have family problems. Christians get cancer.

Do you know one of the good things about not being a pastor? Being able to be human. One time, someone left a brochure critical of a church member on every car in the parking lot.

After the service, as I stood in the receiving line, being nice to and shaking hands with people, someone showed me the brochure. I lost it and used a cuss word!

Then, I realized, after seeing the shocked face of the dear lady standing in front of me, that I had probably caused her to lose her faith.

Do you know what she said? "Steve, you're human too. Quit trying to pretend you aren't." Then, she hugged me.

I don't know much about Benny Hinn (while his hair is different now, in the past, I thought about investing in hairspray!), but I read the other day that a woman got healed in one of his meetings when Hinn wasn't there. When Benny Hinn came out and learned of the healing, he said to the congregation, "That shows how important I was! I was back in the dressing room, fixing my hair." Then, he laughed. I liked Benny Hinn for that because he was quite human.

I believe that there is a correlation between what happens to pagans and what happens to Christians. It is this: Every time a Christian gets hurt, a pagan gets hurt, so the world can see the difference. Every time a pagan has a family problem, a Christian has a family problem, so the world can see the difference. Every time a pagan gets cancer, a Christian gets cancer, so the world can see the difference.

I'm so tired of "Praise the Lord!" Christians, I could scream. Being depressed means that sometimes you simply don't want to praise the Lord. Being human means that too.

Being human also means that you will say stupid things. Not only that, you will do stupid things and think stupid things. That is what it means to be human.

It means that you will feel silly. It means that sometimes you don't want to go to church and won't. Sometimes you will want to cuss and will. That is what it means to be human.

The slogan, "Be patient, God isn't through with me yet" is not only a slogan; it is a truth that every healthy Christian must understand with his or her mind, heart and soul.

Perfection is unattainable in this world. If you think it is, you are going to end up a neurotic Christian. The cartoonist who showed a cannibal pouring the contents of a small box labeled "Instant Missionary" into a big pot is not the only one dreaming. We all dream about instant goodness, instant power and instant perfection. It simply doesn't work that way.

When I was growing up, the sentence I heard probably more than any other was this: "Stephen is not living up to his potential." That was true, of course. It was always true; it is still true; it will always be true (until I become like Him in heaven). There is always more that I could do. I could always be better than I am. I could always love Him more and serve Him better.

The next time someone tells you that you aren't living up to your potential, tell him or her, "Of course, I'm not living up to my potential. And, if it's okay with you, I think I won't live up to it for a while longer!" On the authority of God's Word, I give you permission to be human.

You Have the Right to Be Right

Second, believe it or not, you have the right to be right.

Have I therefore become your enemy because I tell you the truth? (Galatians 4:16)

I spoke at another Christian college a while ago when a student, obviously upset, asked if he could talk to me. As soon as we sat down, he said, "Mr. Brown, I need some help in getting my life straightened out."

I braced myself for a confession about drugs, homosexuality or cheating on exams. What this young man said surprised me: "I have to deal with my arrogance and pride."

I looked at this boy with his head bowed, his spirit broken and his eyes welling up with tears.

I said to him, "Son, you may have a lot of sins, but arrogance is not one of them."

I then asked the student why he thought he was arrogant. He told me about a small group of Christians with whom he met regularly. One of the tenets of the group was total honesty and, the week before, the group had decided to be totally honest with him. In fact, the whole meeting had been devoted to a discussion of what was wrong with this young man. It all boiled down to his arrogant and prideful attitude.

Finally, I looked at the student and asked, "Did you ever think that they may be wrong and you may be right?" From the look on the boy's face, it was obvious he hadn't.

R. C. Sproul, one of the finest Christian writers of our time, was told by a teacher that he couldn't write. That teacher almost robbed us of some great books because, for a long time, R. C. believed her. It is the same with many of us. Time after time, I have seen Christians failing because they believed the turkeys who told them they were dumb.

Maybe you have been told you're dumb. Did you ever think that the people who told you that could be wrong? Perhaps you are afraid to articulate your ideas because you have been told that your ideas aren't worth much. Did you ever think that the idea that your ideas aren't worth much isn't worth much? Perhaps you don't need to apologize all the time. Have you ever considered that one doesn't need to apologize when one is right? Have you ever entertained the idea that you were right?

Tolerance is a good word; but, if we aren't very careful, we can allow tolerance to become a lack of conviction. I believe if I hear one more time, "I'm not a Baptist," (or a Presbyterian or a Methodist), "I'm a Christian," I will scream. Our forefathers called that kind of statement a lack of conviction. Of course, it is more important to be a Christian rather than a member of a denomination, but to suggest that beliefs are not important is just another way of saying, "It doesn't matter what you believe or what your convictions are. Let's just join hands with Jesus and walk off into the sunset together."

There is absolutely nothing sinful about being right. The Law of Averages suggests that, unless you are unusually dumb, you are going to be right at least 50 percent of the time. If you find yourself apologizing most of the time, 50 percent of those times are lies. If you assume you are wrong in every argument, you are lying to yourself at least 50 percent of the time. If you assume that others know better about your life, it is important you remember that you know better about your life at least 50 percent of the time. So, on the authority of God's Word, I give you permission to be right.

You Have the Right to Be Wrong

Third, you not only have the right to be human and to be right, you also have the right to be wrong.

Peter, a Jew, had nothing to do with Gentiles. Once, God gave Peter a vision of all kinds of unclean foods and asked him to eat. The text then reads:

> And a voice came to him, "Rise, Peter; kill and eat." But Peter said, "Not so, Lord! For I have never eaten anything common or unclean." And a voice spoke to him again the second time, "What God has cleansed you must not call common." (Acts 10:13–15)

The Law of Averages suggests that you will be right at least 50 percent of the time. If that is true, the same law suggests that you will be wrong at least 50 percent of the time.

I love the statement by the physics professor. After he finished the course, the professor said to his students, "Fifty percent of everything I have taught you is wrong. My problem is I don't know which 50 percent is wrong!"

Wouldn't it be refreshing to hear that from your pastor, your church leaders, your Christian friends or yourself? On the authority of God's Word, I give you permission to be wrong.

You Have the Right to Fail

Fourth, you have the right to fail.

> Now when Paul and his party set sail from Paphos, they came to Perga in Pamphylia; and John, departing from them, returned to Jerusalem. (Acts 13:13)

That is when John Mark packed everything up. The account continues in Acts 15:37–39:

> Now Barnabas was determined to take with them John called Mark. But Paul insisted that they should not take with them the one who had departed from them in Pamphylia, and had not gone with them to the work. Then the contention became so sharp that they parted from one another. And so Barnabas took Mark and sailed to Cyprus.

But that is not the end of John Mark's story. Take a look at Paul's words in 2 Timothy 4:11, "Only Luke is with me. Get Mark and bring him with you, for he is useful to me for ministry." Mark had failed.

The principle is this: *The only difference between a failure and a success is that the successful person got up the last time he or she failed.*

I heard a commencement speaker say once, "Failure is only in the dictionary of fools and cowards." It was all I could do to keep from jumping up and interrupting his speech with, "That is the dumbest thing I have heard in my life. That is stupid! And I am angry that this college would invite you as the speaker." That guy was a perfectionist, trying to put his trip off on everyone.

Failure is only in the dictionary of fools and cowards? That's crazy! Failure is in everybody's dictionary. I'm going to say it again: A successful person is not the person who doesn't fail. A successful person is the person who got up the last time he or she failed.

I sometimes say to my seminary students when they become really judgmental of other people, "You haven't lived long enough, or sinned big enough or failed nearly enough to know anything about that." On the authority of God's Word, I give you permission to fail.

You Have the Right to Be Offensive

You not only have the right to be human, to be right and wrong and to fail. Fifth, you have the right to be offensive.

> And the rest of the Jews also played the hypocrite with him, so that even Barnabas was carried away with their hypocrisy. But when I saw that they were not straightforward about the truth of the gospel, I said to Peter before them all, "If you, being a Jew, live in the manner of Gentiles and not as the Jews, why do you compel Gentiles to live as Jews?" (Galatians 2:13–14)

Now, what was happening here? Peter the Rock had been a hypocrite . . . and that was even after the resurrection. (That ought to give you an idea just how human people are.) Not only that, Paul was offensive.

Let me tell you something—Christ didn't die to make you nice! Most Christians, at least once a day, ought to offend one person. If that were to happen, we would have to ask forgiveness a lot, but at least we would get honest.

I love Tony Campolo and love to be around him, although I hardly agree with any of his political or sociological views. He often offends people by what he says and I like that even if I think he is wrong. We are brothers. Sometimes, when I hear Tony speak, I find myself thinking, I don't believe he said that! Then, I look at the way Tony is willing to put his views (often offensive to his audience) on the line and I'm proud to be his friend.

Vernon Grounds once said that the trouble with some Christians is they almost say something. I don't know about you, but I'm tired of Christians who almost say something. I like Tony Campolo, Jerry Falwell and others like them because they don't "almost" say something. You know what they believe and think because they are not afraid of being offensive. They remind me of most of the good guys in the Bible.

The fact is, truth almost always offends. Jesus said, "Woe to you when all men speak well of you, for so did their fathers to the false prophets" (Luke 6:26).

I have a beard and have had one before the Flood. But, back when I was a young pastor, I was clean-shaven and baby-faced. One day, I decided to grow a mustache . . . and, to be honest with you, it looked horrible! To make matters worse, this was a long time ago when Christians didn't wear beards or mustaches.

The first day I started growing my mustache, I ran an errand to the post office in my little village on Cape Cod. As soon as I got back to my office, the phone rang and it was one of the dear saints of the church. She asked, "Reverend, what was that I saw on your upper lip?"

I said, "It's a mustache. And I intend on growing a full beard!"

She was absolutely horrified.

Then I said, "Madam, I think you are too fat, but I don't tell you so."

The mustache situation got so bad that people came to my wife, Anna, and asked, "Will you please make him shave it off?" She told them all, "If you don't shut up about it, he is going to have it forever!"

So, finally, I stood in the pulpit of that little church and I said, "I want all of you to know that I'm going to shave off my mustache this afternoon." There was a great sigh of relief from the congregation. "But," I continued, "I want it clearly understood that I'm doing this because I don't like my mustache, not because you don't like it!"

Do you ever say what you really think? Most of us don't. And, as a result of our effort to be nice and sweet, the church has become the most dishonest institution in modern culture. On the authority of God's Word, I give you permission to be offensive.

You Have the Right to Think, Act and Believe as God Leads You

Sixth, you have the right to think, act and believe as God leads you.

> These were more fair-minded than those in Thessalonica, in that they received the word with all readiness, and searched the Scriptures daily to find out whether these things were so. (Acts 17:11)

And, once again, 1 Corinthians 9:3–5:

> My defense to those who examine me is this: Do we have no right to eat and drink? Do we have no right to take along a believing wife, as do also the other apostles, the brothers of the Lord, and Cephas?

> Now the Lord is the Spirit; and where the Spirit of the Lord is, there is liberty. (2 Corinthians 3:17)

> O Corinthians! We have spoken openly to you, our heart is wide open. You are not restricted by us . . . (2 Corinthians 6:11–12)

> Stand fast therefore in the liberty by which Christ has made us free, and do not be entangled again with a yoke of bondage. (Galatians 5:1)

We have always given our daughters the right to think for themselves. Now, they are both Christians, each having a strong walk with Christ. When they were growing up, we encouraged them to express what they felt . . . and that sometimes got us into trouble!

When our younger daughter, Jennifer, was born, my mother and father came to visit and to help out. One day, during that time, our older daughter, Robin, did something wrong. My father picked her up, put her on the couch and said, "Young lady, sit there!" Robin looked back at her grandfather and said, "Why don't you go back to your own home!"

There are times I want to say that to people, but I don't. Sometimes, though, I want to say what I really think. It is easy to think strange thoughts and then censor yourself with, *I must not think this way. What would people say if they knew?* It is easy to act in a way that is silly and improper, and then think to yourself, *I must not act this way; I must be more careful.* It is easy for a thought to come to mind which is not in conformity with Christian doctrine, only to stop yourself with, *I must not think that* or *What would people say if they knew I didn't believe all that?*

Paul makes an interesting comment to the church at Corinth:

> Now I pray to God that you do no evil, not that we should appear approved, but that you should do what is honorable, though we may seem disqualified. For we can do nothing against the truth, but for the truth. (2 Corinthians 13:7–8)

In other words, if you want to think truth, to live truth and to believe truth, truth will eventually become the reality of your life, without the help of someone else who thinks he or she is your mother.

Let me give you a principle: *The genuine can be tested and God will test it so that its genuineness can be proved.* That means, if you think contrary to what God thinks, He is perfectly capable of leading you to proper thinking. If you act in a manner contrary to how God would have you to act, He is perfectly capable of leading you to proper action. If your doctrine is other than His doctrine, He is perfectly capable of leading you to a proper doctrinal position. On the authority of God's Word, I give you permission to think, act and believe as God leads you . . . not as He leads me.

You Have the Right to Be Treated as a Child of God

Seventh, you have the right to be treated as a child of God.

> So God created man in His own image; in the image of God He created him; male and female He created them. (Genesis 1:27)

Therefore I write these things being absent, lest being present I should use sharpness, according to the authority which the Lord has given me for edification and not for destruction. (2 Corinthians 13:10)

The entire New Testament gives witness to the responsibility of Christians to treat other Christians (and even pagans) with great respect and integrity. When other Christians don't do that to you, that is as much a sin as it would be if you didn't do that to them.

I think it was Leo Durocher, one of baseball's greatest and most controversial managers, who, in a ball game, patiently bore the taunts of a heckler in the stands.

Finally, she yelled, "If I were your wife, I would feed you poison!"

Durocher looked up and said, "Lady, if I were your husband, I would drink it!"

One time, Winston Churchill was approached by a woman who said to him, "Mr. Prime Minister, you are drunk."

He replied, "Madam, you are quite correct. But you are ugly and, in the morning, I will be sober."

You do no favor to other Christians when you accept their lack of respect and honor, as if you deserved it. There are many arrogant, elitist, insensitive clods in the Body of Christ. The reason there are so many is because we mealy-mouth Christians have not held them accountable for their actions. On the authority of God's Word, I give you permission to hold them accountable. You have the right to be treated as a child of God.

You Have the Right to Not Like Everybody

You not only have the right to be human, to be right and wrong, to fail, to be offensive, to follow God's leading and to be treated as a child of God. Finally, you have the right to not like everybody.

Then the contention became so sharp that they parted from one another . . . (Acts 15:39)

I could wish that those who trouble you would even cut themselves off! (Galatians 5:12)

Will Rogers said, "I never met a man I didn't like." On the broadcast, I once said that Rogers lied and got a bunch of critical letters! They may have been right; I don't know Will Rogers's heart, but I still believe he lied.

Have you ever met someone that you just couldn't stand? Those who say they haven't will probably lie about other things as well. As a matter of fact, you don't have to like everybody. As a matter of fact, you won't like everybody. Now, you don't have the right to treat anyone horribly or to act in an unloving way; you must treat others with honor, but you have the right to not like certain people.

I once had a man working for me that I just couldn't stand. I mean, when he walked through the door, I found myself getting angry. I was young then and thought that, before I could fire him, I had to first love (like) him. I would get on my knees and pray about it, think that I had it settled and then, the man would come into my office and I would get ticked again. (That man never understood that he kept his job by irritating me!)

Finally, things got so bad, the institutional problems became so great and the church began to go down the tube—all because of the actions of this man. Eventually, an elder said to me, "Steve, fire him now and love him later." I did and it was one of the best decisions I ever made. And, yes, I learned to love him.

On the authority of God's Word, I give you permission to not like some people.

Some People Don't Like Free Christians

Fourth and finally, a Christian philosophy of boldness should not only include a Christian model, a Creator's responsibility and a believer's rights. It should also include the reality that some people, including Christians, simply don't like free Christians.

We have seen some of these verses before, but let me give them to you again in the context of what we are learning right now.

In the Galatian church, after teaching the doctrine of liberty and freedom, Paul discovers that some religious folks have come into the church, undermining the freedom that he taught. Paul says this,

> O foolish Galatians! Who has bewitched you that you should not obey the truth, before whose eyes Jesus Christ was clearly portrayed among you as crucified? This only I want to learn from you: Did you receive the Spirit by the works of the law, or by the hearing of faith? Are you so foolish? Having begun in the Spirit, are you now being made perfect by the flesh? (Galatians 3:1–3)

> So then, brethren, we are not children of the bondwoman but of the free. Stand fast therefore in the liberty by which Christ has made us free, and do not be entangled again with the yoke of bondage. (Galatians 4:31–5:1)

> You ran well. Who hindered you from obeying the truth? This persuasion does not come from Him who calls you. (Galatians 5:7–8)

> I could wish that those who trouble you would even cut themselves off [emasculate themselves]! (Galatians 5:12)

Paul is not predisposed to be nice and gentle to turkeys who rob God's people of their freedom!

Let me tell you something that you should remember: If you become a free Christian, there are other Christians who are not going to like you. They will try to force you into their particular mold. They will judge you and become angry. Never mind, though. Their basic presupposition or error is that they think they are your mother . . . and they are not. Remember that.

A number of years ago, we took our daughters to Washington. We wanted them to see something of our country and what makes it great. Our mistake was that we took them to Congress on the day they debated a big spending bill. Anyway, I had always thought that our leaders seemed to do some stupid things, but that they had some information I didn't have. After all, they were our leaders. I always thought that they could be wrong, but that they knew what they were doing. I'll let you in on a little, frightening secret—they don't know any more than the rest of us!

In an episode of the television show *Barney Miller*, the plain clothes cops were required to wear uniforms for awhile. One of the characters said to Barney, "The thing that bothers me is that, if we put on a uniform, it will look like we know what we're doing. Then, we will think that we know what we're doing. And then, we will be in trouble!"

Let me tell you something: Other people don't know any more than you know. They don't have the right to tell you what to do. If you are free, be free. Don't let anyone rob you of that freedom.

In the early days of Key Life, we hired a lot of consultants. The greatest lesson I learned in those early days was that they didn't know any more than we did!

Learn that lesson about others too. Don't put anybody up on a pedestal. Make sure you remember the simple, frightening truth: They don't know any more than you do.

4

A Profile

Seven Reasons Christians Lack Boldness

Knowing that we have a problem with boldness and freedom, and understanding its philosophy, provide an important basis . . . but they don't get at the root. The real question is: Why aren't we, as Christians, bold and free? In answer, I want us to examine a profile of boldness: The seven reasons Christians lack boldness.

Sometimes when you analyze things, you can then deal with them. That is certainly true of anxiety. Let me give you a principle that has nothing to do with freedom, but will help you with fear: Undefined fear is a bear . . . Defined fear is a teddy bear.

Just so, being a wimp can often be attributed to the fact that the wimp syndrome is never analyzed. How many times have you asked yourself the following:

Why am I such a pushover?
Why didn't I tell him what I really thought?
Why did I say "yes" when I meant to say "no"?

The fact is, knowing what is wrong is fairly easy, but knowing why something is wrong is not so easy.

Look at what Paul says in 2 Corinthians 13:5: "Examine yourselves as to whether you are in the faith. Prove yourselves. Do you not know yourselves, that Jesus Christ is in you?"

So, let's do some examination. I have seven reasons Christians lack boldness. In each case, I'm going to give you the problem and the biblical solution.

Insecurity

First, Christians lack boldness because of insecurity. In other words, because of the guilt which causes insecurity. If we don't do anything about our guilt, it makes us think that we deserve nothing but denunciation, condemnation, accusation and blame. People who know they're forgiven and free are quite bold. People who are always guilty are constantly hovering in a corner, whining about how horrible they are. That is an abomination to God. And furthermore, it is taking lightly the blood of Christ.

The process is this: In order to come to Christ, Christians are forced to understand sin and guilt. The only requirement for becoming a Christian is to *not* be good enough to become a Christian. We are radically sinful and, as such, the only way we can be saved is through the grace and mercy of God mediated through the blood of Christ. And so, there is a sense in which Christians are more aware of their sin and the resulting guilt than anybody else in the world. Therefore, when you are put down, thought of as being a wimp and looked down upon, you think you deserve it.

What is the solution? Take a look at your position, as a Christian, in Scripture:

There is therefore now no condemnation to those who are in Christ Jesus, who do not walk according to the flesh, but according to the Spirit. (Romans 8:1)

For we do not have a High Priest who cannot sympathize with our weaknesses, but was in all points tempted as we are, yet without sin. Let us therefore come boldly to the throne of grace, that we may obtain mercy and find grace to help in time of need. (Hebrews 4:15–16)

And as it is appointed for men to die once, but after this the judgment, so Christ was offered once to bear the sins of many . . . (Hebrews 9:27–28)

Let us draw near with a true heart in full assurance of faith, having our hearts sprinkled from an evil conscience and our bodies washed with pure water. Let us hold fast the confession of our hope without wavering, for He who promised is faithful. (Hebrews 10:22–23)

I believe that Christians spend too much time trying to do God's will and too little time accepting God's love. If you don't feel forgiven, accepted and loved by God, don't try to help Him, because your help will simply hinder. God doesn't need your help. He needs you to know that you are forgiven and free.

The day I knew that I was forgiven was the day I turned mean. (Okay, "mean" may not be the word!) It was, though, the day I stopped groveling before other human beings.

I once worked for a church in Boston where there were two problems. The first problem was that they articulated the need to have more young people at the church. The second problem was that the power of the church rested solely on the church trustees. In fact, the pastor went to a trustee meeting by invitation only.

To solve the first problem, I had a basketball hoop put up in the church parking lot. One evening, I met with the president of the board of trustees who told me, as we stood in the parking lot, that he intended to take down the basketball hoop because it would only attract the "riffraff" in the neighborhood. Usually, I would have said, "Let's talk about it and do the Christlike thing about this." Instead, I told the president of the trustees that it would be a cold day in a hot place before he took down the hoop.

He simply turned and walked away from me. I promptly followed him . . . right into a trustee meeting where I was not invited. I was still yelling when I realized where I was. The president of the board, realizing that he had a bad situation on his hands, said to the trustees, who at this moment, became as quiet as mice, "The pastor and I have had a small disagreement, but we will work it out between ourselves. Meanwhile, the pastor is at our meeting tonight by my invitation."

That is when I lost it. I said, "Jack, I'm not here by your invitation. I'm here at the invitation of Christ because He made me the pastor of this church and, as such, responsible for everything which goes on here, including trustee meetings. From now on, I will be at all of these meetings . . . at His invitation, not Jack's!" And I was.

Shortly thereafter, the president of the board of trustees, trying to intimidate me the way he had all the pastors in the past, said, "Pastor, I was shocked at your behavior." I told him that he should not have been and that I was capable of far worse.

I almost scared myself to death. But, you know something, that was when I was forgiven. People who know they're forgiven are quite bold. Once you know you're forgiven absolutely, accepted absolutely and loved absolutely, groveling isn't the issue anymore. The basketball hoop becomes the issue, not your sin. You don't have to feel insecure.

Insincerity

Second, Christians lack boldness because of insincerity and hypocrisy. The problem is this: If you have a great need to be loved, you will even lie to get it. When you have a need to be liked and accepted, you will certainly avoid making any waves. So, we are not truthful with people. We tell them what they want to hear. We tell them what they want to know. The problem is, as a result, we may be loved, *but we won't be respected.*

The solution can be found in Paul's letters to the Corinthians.

> But with me it is a very small thing that I should be judged by you or by a human court. In fact, I do not even judge myself. (1 Corinthians 4:3)

Therefore we make it our aim, whether present or absent, to be well pleasing to Him. (2 Corinthians 5:9)

But "he who glories, let him glory in the Lord." For not he who commends himself is approved, but whom the Lord commends. (2 Corinthians 10:17–18)

C. S. Lewis wrote a very insightful essay entitled "The Inner Ring" in which he talks about how most of us want to be a part of the in-group and would, in fact, do almost anything to achieve that end. Lewis writes:

The quest of the inner ring will break your hearts unless you break it. But if you break it, a surprising result will follow. If in your working hours you make the work your end, you will presently find yourself all unawares inside the only circle in your profession that really matters. You will be one of the sound craftsmen, and other sound craftsmen will know it.[10]

The principle is this: *When you do things to be accepted and loved, you will achieve just the opposite. When you do things because they are right, you will be accepted and loved by those who matter.*

I have found that almost everything of importance in this world is a side-benefit of something else. Do you want happiness? Chase it and it eludes you. Don't look for happiness. Just do what you're supposed to do and, then, happiness will follow along like a tail behind a dog. Quit worrying about being accepted. Instead, be true to yourself. The side-benefit, believe it or not, is acceptance.

Inaccuracy

Third, Christians lack boldness because of inaccuracy: We use the wrong models; selecting nice, bland people rather than strong, good people.

Mother Teresa is not the only model of Christianity that we should accept. It seems that, sometimes, we lift before the people of God only those who are humble, quiet, bland and nice. As a result, we come to think that "real" Christians are humble, quiet, bland and nice. Whenever we aren't humble, quiet, bland and nice, we feel something less than a Christian. So, we work hard to be humble, quiet, bland and nice.

The solution is found in Acts 4:13:

> Now when they saw the boldness of Peter and John, and perceived that they were uneducated and untrained men, they marveled. And they realized that they had been with Jesus.

In David Mains's book *The Rise of the Religion of Antichristism*, Donald Wildmon, executive director of the National Federation for Decency, is quoted as saying, "In seven years of monitoring television, I have not seen one program, cast in a modern day setting, in which one person depicted as a Christian was shown as a warm, compassionate, intelligent person." Mains goes on to add his commentary:

> I'm not opposed to drama or humor or art or literature or the real-life situations that these forms so adequately present. But when Christians are regularly shown as wimpy, lackluster, two-faced, and mindless, with none of the courage or beauty or goodness or intellect that we know the church represents, I say there is a bias that needs to be called to account. And the accusing term to use is "antichristism."[11]

After studying the Bible for years and being a student of church history, I was absolutely blown away by the models that God has given His people to follow and to copy. The problem is that, much of the time, we follow the wrong models.

Did you hear about the man who ordered plans from a certain company to build a birdhouse? When the plans arrived and the man tried to put together the birdhouse, he discovered a mistake . . . the company had sent him plans for a sailboat. The man wrote to the company, explaining the problem and, in return, received a letter of apology. The company explained that there was a mix-up of orders and that it would be quickly corrected. In the last paragraph, the company's letter explained that they had sent his birdhouse plans to a man in California who had ordered plans for a sailboat. They wrote, "If you think you have it bad, think of that man. There is a man in California, trying to sail a very weird boat!"

That is the mistake we make.

Not too long ago, I attended an ecclesiastical meeting. During lunch, I sat down at a table where some rather vocal feminists were discussing their feelings on the rearing of children.

One of the women said that she was against guns; so, she had decided the only toys she was going to give her son were dolls.

The other women agreed.

Another woman said that she had not only taken the toy guns away from her two sons, she had also forbidden them to be involved in competitive sports. She said, "I feel that aggression, no matter what form it takes, is the result of training, and I am going to train my children to be different."

Now, I'm not in the business of making a case for toy guns and competitive sports. I was, however, depressed after that lunch. I felt sorry for those boys because they were being brought up with a false view of reality. I got the distinct impression that the only reality they would ever know was "they will be nice to you if you will be nice to them."

Only the person wearing "rose-colored glasses" believes that we live in a world in which all differences can be resolved calmly and rationally. Not only that, nice people sit down and talk out their problems.

That distorted picture carries over into our Christianity. Christians are to be nice and bland. May God have mercy on us if the blood of Christ was shed and the only result is niceness. I am reminded of H. Richard Niebuhr's comment about modern Christianity and its theology of "a God without wrath who brought men without sin into a kingdom without judgment through the ministrations of a Christ without a cross."

The Christian faith recognizes the aggressiveness of the world. It creates heroes and heroines who will not bend, break, or compromise. It teaches that there is a lusty, materialistic paganism out to eat us alive unless we find something better than pious platitudes and nice news.

Let's look at the record. The fact is, most of the men and women of the Bible and church history would be uncomfortable with our bland religion. Abraham, Isaac and Jacob would wince to see what we have done with what they started. Moses would get angry enough to find some stone tablets to break. Joshua might call out his fearless and godly troops, fighting to give the land back to the pagans. Gideon, Deborah and Samson would wonder who was leading, and the prophets would laugh. John the Baptist would never get invited to dinner—and would be glad. Peter would question where the Christians went. Priscilla and Lydia would make jokes about the silly, costless Christianity they saw, and Paul would blush. And God, who wants His people to be far more earthy, bold, and real than the pagans, must find that the cross at the center of His heart hurts more than it did before.

The first miracle Jesus performed was at a wedding party. At that celebration, He turned the water into wine (see John 2). Someone has suggested that modern-day Christianity is busy turning the wine back into water. That is true. We have taken what was a very real and exciting gift, making it into something so bland that most of the people who first received the gift wouldn't be able to recognize it.

In Exodus 34, Moses renewed the covenant with the people of God. While Moses was up on the mountain, receiving the law of God, Aaron and the people made a golden idol, in front of which they fell down and worshiped. When Moses came down from the mountain to discover what was going on, he didn't go off into a corner and whine. He didn't cry out, "Mercy teacups!" He didn't talk about love and forgiveness. He got angry—really angry.

There were consequences of their disobedience, but eventually God renewed the covenant with His people. Among other things, God said to Moses:

Behold, I make a covenant. Before all your people I will do marvels such as have not been done in all the earth, nor in any nation; and all the people among whom you are shall see the work of the Lord. For it is an awesome thing that I will do with you. (Exodus 34:10)

"An awesome thing" God does with His people. When was the last time you heard the word *awesome* used to describe the people of God and what He had done with them?

As you read through the Scripture, you will find sinful, dishonest and fearful men and women . . . but you will not find weak men and women.

Consider Joshua, the great fighter for God. When he was called, it was because a man he loved and followed had died. One would expect that Joshua would simply fall apart. But he didn't! Listen to what God said to Joshua:

Moses My servant is dead. Now therefore, arise, go over this Jordan, you and all this people, to the land which I am giving to them— the children of Israel. Every place that the sole of your foot will tread upon I have given you, as I said to Moses. From the wilderness and this Lebanon as far as the great river, the River Euphrates, all the land of the Hittites, and to the Great Sea toward the going down of the sun, shall be your territory. No man shall be able to stand before you all the days of your life; as I was with Moses, so I will be with you. I will not leave you nor forsake you. Be strong and of good courage . . . (Joshua 1:2–6)

What follows is a story of great courage, strength and commitment. Nobody laughed at Joshua.

In the Old Testament, take a look at the judges of Israel. They march across the pages of Scripture, leaving fire in their wake. If you are looking for weak and insipid folks, don't look at Deborah, Othniel, Gideon or Samson.

When the last judge, Samuel, spoke, people listened because "all Israel from Dan to Beersheba knew that Samuel had been established as a prophet of the Lord" (1 Samuel 3:20). How did they know? They didn't know because Samuel was soft and gentle. They knew because God's power was clear in his life.

Consider David. David was not always good, but he was strong. "So David went on and became great, and the Lord God of hosts was with him" (2 Samuel 5:10). David's God made him strong.

While we're making a list, let's not forget to include Elijah on Mount Carmel. One man, God's man, against 450 prophets of Baal. In 1 Kings 18, Elijah makes fun of the prophets of Baal when their god didn't bother to answer their prayers:

> Cry aloud, for he is a god; either he is meditating, or he is busy, or he is on a journey, or perhaps he is sleeping and must be awakened. (v. 27)

Today, many people might judge Elijah as intolerant and arrogant. God judged him as being faithful.

And what about Ezra and Nehemiah? They were builders, fighters and leaders. Against overwhelming odds, they were willing to stand up and be counted.

Also strong leaders, the prophets all needed a course in tact! Just reading their words is enough to make us wince. Listen to Amos speaking the word of God:

> I hate, I despise your feast days, and I do not savor your sacred assemblies. Though you offer Me burnt offerings and your grain offerings, I will not accept them, nor will I regard your fattened peace offerings. Take away from Me the noise of your songs, for I will not hear the melody of your stringed instruments. But let justice run down like water, and righteousness like a mighty stream. (Amos 5:21–24)

The prophets would be uncomfortable in the company of nice Christians.

The New Testament won't yield any models for our soft and insipid Christianity either. Can you imagine John the Baptist as a part of the Evangelical jet set? His clothes simply would not fit in with the well-dressed clergyman's image. His voice thundered judgment, his demeanor frightened and his food of locusts—Yuk! John the Baptist just won't do. Peter the Rock; James and John, the sons of thunder; Paul, the bold rabbi—all of them were gutsy Christians who made the world tremble.

Listen to Paul's sarcasm as he writes to the people at Corinth:

> Now I, Paul, myself am pleading with you by the meekness and gentleness of Christ—who in presence am lowly among you, but being absent am bold toward you. But I beg you that when I am present I may not be bold with that confidence by which I intend to be bold against some, who think of us as if we walked according to the flesh. (2 Corinthians 10:1–2)

You won't find Jesus as a model of weakness either. We have made Him nice and sweet . . . and He isn't. He was gentle, but His gentleness was only a part of the picture. Listen to His words:

> Woe to you, scribes and Pharisees, hypocrites! For you are like whitewashed tombs which indeed appear beautiful outwardly, but inside are full of dead men's bones and all uncleanness. Even so you also outwardly appear righteous to men, but inside you are full of hypocrisy and lawlessness. Woe to you, scribes and Pharisees, hypocrites! Because you build the tombs of the prophets and adorn the monuments of the righteous, and say, "If we had lived in the days of our fathers, we would not have been partakers with them in the blood of the prophets." Therefore you are witnesses against yourselves that you are sons of those who murdered the prophets. Fill up, then, the measure of your fathers' guilt. Serpents, brood of vipers! How can you escape the condemnation of hell? (Matthew 23:27–33)

Wherever we got our idea of the Christian as a sweet servant, we certainly didn't get it from the Bible. We didn't get it from church history either.

As you look through the history of the church of Christ since the first century, you will find that the men and women who gave us our heritage were also strong, earthy, committed and bold

Christians. Those people haunt my dreams and capture my imagination. Sometimes when I close my eyes at night, I can hear the cries of the martyrs and the curses of the adversaries. I can picture the men and women who have stood up to the world without bending, breaking or compromising.

I can see Irenaeus, during the last quarter of the second century, serving as Bishop of Lyons where his predecessor, Pothinus, died at the hand of Marcus Aurelius. His strength and power turned almost an entire population to Christ, and his most famous work *Against Heresies* was a bold statement defending the Christian faith.

I think of Origen (c. A.D. 185–c. 254), who watched his father, Leonidas, die for his faith in Christ and who stood strong and bold for the rest of his life, only to face torture and finally death at the hands of those who could not abide his courageous strength.

Chrysostom (A.D. 347–407) attacked every social and spiritual evil of his time and, for his boldness, was sent into exile, where he died broken in body, but not in spirit. Augustine (A.D. 354–430), a contemporary of Chrysostom, was one of the most earthy Christians Jesus ever called. When told of the fall of Rome, he was sad, but commented to the effect that, while he was a citizen of Rome, he was also a citizen of a city that would never fall. You can read about it in his book *City of God*.

Listen to some of Augustine's "soft" words spoken to those who had been spared in the fall of Rome because they called themselves Christians:

> Therefore ought they to give God thanks, and with sincere confession flee for refuge to His name, that so they may escape the punishment of eternal fire—they who with lying lips took upon them this name, that they might escape the punishment of present destruction. For of those whom you see insolently and shamelessly insulting the servants of Christ, there are numbers who would not have escaped that destruction and slaughter had they not pretended that they themselves were Christ's servants. Yet now, in ungrateful pride and most impious madness, and at the risk of being punished in everlasting darkness, they perversely oppose that name

under which they fraudulently protected themselves for the sake of enjoying the light of this brief life.[12]

The sermons of Bernard of Clairvaux (A.D. 1090–1153) ought to be read by every Christian who thinks that "sweet" and "Christian" go together. One biographer of Bernard said of him, "Bernard was a man of humility, but one who spoke with great conviction when convinced that he was right; he never apologized for his message."[13]

The list grows long and the space is limited, but don't forget Luther standing at Worms. His message was certainly not your typical "Let's be friends and love Jesus" appeal. He said, when asked to recant on penalty of excommunication, "Here I stand, I can do no other, so help me God!"

I think of Peter Cartwright, an early American Methodist pioneer preacher. It is said that when he approached a town he would often stand on a hill above the town and those with him would hear him say, "I smell hell!" Such language!

Our past is ripe with models of strength, boldness and courage. Gregory, Theodora, Savonarola, Beza, Ridley, Latimer, Zwingli, Wesley, Whitfield, Zinzendorf, the Countess of Huntingdon, Newton, Edwards, Mather and Moody all walk in my dreams. Sometimes I can hear the scorn and the Scripture falling from the lips of the Scottish Covenanters and the French Huguenots as they went to their deaths. In my dreams, I hear the crackle of the flames and the blows of the hammers as they went Home to be with Christ.

Revivalist Billy Sunday's words, while perhaps not as eloquent as Spurgeon's or as deep as Calvin's, ring out over the heritage of the church: "I'm against sin. I'll kick it as long as I've got a foot, and I'll fight it as long as I've got a fist. I'll butt it as long as I've got a head. I'll bite it as long as I've got a tooth. When I'm old and fistless and footless and toothless, I'll gum it till I go home to glory and it goes home to perdition!"

Our heritage as believers has been sold for a mess of pottage. God, at least in the past, has not been in the business of creating wimps. Given the fact that He doesn't change His mind, it is easy to construct a syllogism. Premise: God has not, in the past, created wimps. Premise: God doesn't change His mind. Conclusion: God isn't creating wimps now. We are called to be bold, free believers.

Stop using nice people as your model. Use good people . . . but not nice ones.

Inhibition

Christians lack boldness not only because of insecurity, insincerity and inaccuracy. Fourth, they lack boldness because of inhibition and propriety. The problem is this: There are certain things a Christian shouldn't do. A Christian should never burp at a funeral, chatter during a prayer, laugh at a mistake, and say anything except for nice, mild comments. A Christian should never get angry, speak out of turn or disagree with a leader. A Christian should never question authority or ask for an explanation. Questions should not be asked and doubts should never be expressed. It simply isn't done.

The solution is Matthew 15:1–3:

> Then the scribes and Pharisees who were from Jerusalem came to Jesus, saying, "Why do Your disciples transgress the tradition of the elders? For they do not wash their hands when they eat bread." He answered and said to them, "Why do you also transgress the commandment of God because of your tradition?"

You may know the old story about an elderly lady who, for the first time, attended the worship service of a very formal church. She listened to the hymns of praise . . . and wanted to shout. She listened to the preacher preach . . . and wanted to say "Amen!" As the service progressed, the elderly woman restrained herself by holding on to the pew in front of her until her knuckles turned white.

When she just couldn't remain silent any longer, the woman jumped up and shouted, "Praise the Lord!"

An usher came up to her and said, "Madam, you simply can't do that in here."

The statement "It just isn't done" always requires a question: "Why isn't it done?" If there is no answer . . . *Do it anyway.*

I was never one to pray for revival when I was a pastor. Do you know why? Because you can't control a revival. People are apt to say a lot of things that won't be doctrinally correct and theologically proper. If you say and think the expected, you are not dealing with the Spirit of Christ. *Proper* is just another word for *control.*

David Augsburger said that we learn conformity almost from the cradle. He points out that everyone is born an original, but dies a copy and that whom you copy determines your destiny.

When you copy Jesus, He enhances the original . . . because He didn't make a mistake in the first place.

Instinct

Fifth, Christians lack boldness because of instinct. In other words, we have past problems, dysfunctional experiences and a lost child. As a result, we have not developed proper instincts. The problem is this: We have something in our background which has caused us to have a great need to please, to be a rescuer and to compromise.

Perhaps you were abandoned and are now afraid that people will abandon you if you get out of line. Perhaps you have generational guilt or irrational fears. Perhaps your parents always fought and you were constantly placed in between. Perhaps there has been abuse. Perhaps there is family shame.

For whatever reason, the demons of our past, the secrets we have never told, cause us to remain quiet when we should speak, to say "yes" when we ought to say "no," and to act sweet when all we want to do is to spit.

The solution:

Therefore, if anyone is in Christ, he is a new creation; old things have passed away; behold, all things have become new. (2 Corinthians 5:17)

It is important to analyze the reason for our feelings and, once that analysis is made, to act on what we know and *not* on what we feel. It is one thing to know why you do something that is wimpish; it is quite another thing to stop it.

At this point, it is well to remember the reality of your life, not the background from which you have come. You are now a new creature in Christ. You are a child of the King. Act like it and eventually your feelings will catch up with the reality of who you are. Not only that, it can be quite addicting.

Remember that you are not controlled by your past. Fake it until you make it. Act as if your past were not so horrible and the present will erase the past with the reality of your new life in Christ.

Instruction

Sixth, Christians lack boldness because of instruction—bad teaching. The problem is expressed in a letter I received from a woman whose mother recently died. I quote it with a bit of pride:

> I started receiving your tapes where I lived in 1985 when I moved home to care for my 88 and 90-year-old parents. After I'd shown much enthusiasm for your tapes, my mother started listening to them in 1989. When she moved in with my sister, they ordered their own tapes and Mama listened to each over and over. Mama had suffered a major stroke in 1987 so was confined to a wheelchair and had to learn to eat and write with her left hand. Each evening my sister set up a table, next to Mama's hospital bed, with a tape recorder and one of your tapes. The first thing each morning she listened for 15 minutes to your tape.
>
> One visit I made, Mama asked me a personal question and then told me to say "Shut up!" if I didn't want to answer. My jaw dropped. I'd had my mouth washed out with soap for saying that as a child. Mama laughed and said, "Are you surprised? I'm free of lots of old rules since I've listened to Steve Brown. What he teaches is refreshing."
>
> Mama was free . . . At 92 she was more full of humor, less prudish and less tied to collections of petty prejudices than in her entire life. She said also that she wanted to continue to grow.

My mother had been raised in a very legalistic church. My father's father was a pastor and Mama and my father were married 67 years. They raised us five children to strict Victorian standards. We all chafed against that during our growing years.

On October 18 this year, Mama died after only two days of illness. Her last well morning, she listened to your tape. By that night she was in a coma. I know she is continuing her prayers for you as she and my father dance around heaven as they were never allowed to do in this life. May God bless you as you continue in His work of telling people the gospel which frees and saves. Thank God and you for that.

That is a high and holy compliment . . .

At a church I served for a number of years, we had an elderly pastor who had, all of his life, lived under the structures, not only of being a pastor, but also of a very legalistic church. Because our church was quite open and honest, my pastor friend went through culture shock. He told me one day, "Steve, I feel like I'm living a new life."

The problem in both of those cases is the problem of bad teaching. *Institutions will always, if left unchecked, move toward constraint and control.* The teachers will teach that which will keep the troops in line.

What is the solution of bad teaching? You will find it in Galatians 1:6–8:

> I marvel that you are turning away so soon from Him who called you in the grace of Christ, to a different gospel, which is not another, but there are some who trouble you and want to pervert the gospel of Christ. But even if we, or an angel from heaven, preach any other gospel to you than what we have preached to you, let him be accursed.

How do you counter bad teaching? You do it with truth.

One of the things you will find happening as you become a bold, free Christian is that you will immediately feel guilty. A lot of that will come from inside you . . . but a lot of it will come from those who, without knowing, would rob you of your boldness with what they believe to be Bible doctrine. You need to counter the lies with the truth. You need to become a teacher yourself.

Intimidation

Finally, not only do Christians lack boldness because of insecurity, insincerity, inaccuracy, inhibition, instinct and instruction, they lack boldness because of the intimidation of power-hungry leaders.

One of the major problems in the church is that leaders tend to want to control their followers. Now, I believe that leaders should lead, but I also believe that you owe no man or woman your soul. The neurotic tendency of power is that it is a growing monster. The more it eats, the bigger it gets.

I have a friend who was discipled by an older man. As he grew in Christ, my friend became a mature, thinking and acting Christian. Recently, he made a decision that was contrary to the will of the man who discipled him. My friend wrote to tell me of the man's anger, "Steve, I didn't understand why he was so angry. But I've been thinking about it, and I have decided that, because he discipled me, he feels betrayed when I act contrary to his decision. I have confronted him with what I believe to be true . . . but he is still angry. I don't know what to do."

Leaders should raise up people so that they can stand on their own and, as a result, become leaders themselves. Let me give you a solution to the problem.

> Moreover I call God as witness against my soul, that to spare you I came no more to Corinth. Not that we have dominion over your faith, but are fellow workers for your joy; for by faith you stand. (2 Corinthians 1:23–24)

> The elders who are among you I exhort, I who am a fellow elder and a witness of the sufferings of Christ, and also a partaker of the glory that will be revealed. (1 Peter 5:1)

When Robin came home from college, she lived with us for about seven months. During that time, I got back into the role of the sovereign father. On one occasion, when I yelled at her about something, she simply turned and walked away. I was quite angry and said, "Young lady, you come back in here!" Robin did; but, as she came back, I realized what had happened.

I said to her, "Robin, I'm not going to treat you like that again. It is hard for a father to realize when his daughter is grown up." Then, I began to cry. And then, Robin began to cry.

She said, "Dad, this is the first time I've ever seen you cry . . . " From that day on, our relationship has been different and right.

Those kinds of confrontations need to take place regularly among Christians. We need to say to those who would control and manipulate, "I'm just not going to allow you to do that anymore." That will be good for you and it will be good for them. The solution to intimidation is for us to learn to grow and to stand on our own. Once we do, we are free.

For some reason, we have taken the plain teaching of Jesus on servant leadership—of being equal before God—and have turned it into a structure that is not that different from General Motors.

Let me show you what the Head of the Church says:

> You know that the rulers of the Gentiles lord it over them, and those who are great exercise authority over them. Yet it shall not be so among you; but whoever desires to become great among you, let him be your servant. And whoever desires to be first among you, let him be your slave—just as the Son of Man did not come to be served, but to serve, and to give His life a ransom for many. (Matthew 20:25–28)

5

Problem #1

Guilt, the Great Manipulator

We have just uncovered the seven reasons Christians lack boldness. More specifically, though, there are two problems the Christian encounters in his or her transformation into the bold and free believer. The first is guilt, the great manipulator. The second is fear, the bane of boldness. (We will look at that in the next chapter.) Now, before we get to the problem of guilt, you need to understand the soil out of which it grows: Legalism.

When asked for a simple definition of the term *neurotic*, a famous psychiatrist once said, "A neurotic is a person who cannot say 'damn.'"[14] I probably ought not say this, but I believe there is more truth in that than most Christians would think. There are certain taboos among Christians that reflect neurotic guilt. I am by no means suggesting that we ought to use "damn" more often. However, I am suggesting that whatever it is that makes Christians think that saying "damn" is a major aberration of God's law has become a bonanza for the manipulators of God's people—and that situation makes me angry.

You can find those taboos almost everywhere. For instance, what will happen if you don't have your devotions tomorrow morning? Is it possible, do you think, that you will get the fever and die? A friend of mine who has an office in downtown Dallas told me that, one morning, a friend of his entered his office and asked in a panic, "Do you have a Bible?" He allowed that he did. And his friend said, "Thank God. I forgot to read the Bible this morning, and I couldn't go to work without reading my Bible."

Let it not be said that I am against Bible reading. I advocate the practice from the pulpit, in my personal counseling and on the radio broadcast. However, I do not advocate it because it is some kind of magic formula whereby God rears back and passes a "blessing miracle" on you because you read the Bible for the day. The daily Bible reading should be a time when you listen to the Father. If it becomes an act of magic to keep you from getting hurt during the day, there is a great danger that the manipulators are going to "clean your clock."

A church I once served had a ministry in the arts. We often had concerts and plays in our sanctuary that could not be described as strictly Christian. For instance, some of the concerts were secular jazz concerts and some of the plays were the same plays that you would find at your local center for the performing arts. Occasionally, we had a creative dance in one of our worship services. We did not go into this ministry without much thought and prayer. We came to the conclusion that the problem with most Americans is not that they don't think about Jesus. The problem is that they don't think about anything. Our arts program was an effort to get people to think—with the hope that, if they started thinking, maybe then we could get them to think specifically about Jesus.

During this time, I was teaching part of a leadership course in a Christian college. One of the students who was from our city asked some hostile questions during a question and answer period. I wasn't sure why he was angry at me until after the class. He came up to me and said, "Pastor Brown, the last time I was home on vacation I visited your church and I don't think your church is biblical."

"I'm accused of a lot of things," I said, "but 'not being biblical' is usually not one of them. If you'll tell me where we've been unbiblical, I'll see that we change."

"When I was home I went to your church for a concert," the student said, his voice and demeanor becoming more and more intense as he talked. "I was glad, because I was looking for something that would lift my spirits and turn my thoughts toward God. When I got there, I was horrified that it was not a Christian concert; but, rather, a worldly concert. I just think that you have a responsibility to honor God in what you do. Jazz does not honor God. If I had wanted to listen to jazz, I would have gone to a bar."

"I'm sorry you were offended," I said, "but I think your offense is founded in your cultural likes and dislikes—not in the Bible. However, if you can show me where the Bible says that we shouldn't have jazz concerts, I will stop them."

The student's face went absolutely blank. Nobody had ever asked him specifically where the Bible confirmed his legalism. He stammered and stuttered, trying to think of a verse that wasn't there.

I said to him, "Son, would you like me to tell you why jazz concerts are biblical?" He agreed that that would be good if I could do it. So, I showed him where Jubal was the father of all those (both Christian and pagan) who play the harp and the flute (Genesis 4:21). I showed him how we are commanded to praise God with the "sound" of the trumpet, the stringed instruments and the flutes (Psalm 150:3–4). I pointed out that David and all of Israel "played music before the Lord on all kinds of instruments made of fir wood, on harps, on stringed instruments, on tambourines, on sistrums, and on cymbals" (2 Samuel 6:5).

"Let me ask you a question," I said. "Would you tell me what is Christian about the musical note A?" He looked puzzled as I continued, "To be perfectly honest with you, there is nothing particularly Christian about the note A except that that note was created by God. When a Christian plays the note A and he or she does it well, whether that note is found in a hymn or in a piece of jazz, it becomes a Christian's offering to God. And that is why we have jazz concerts in our church."

My young friend said that he would think about it. I'm glad, because Christians need to think. Legalism (i.e., that kind of Christianity that measures faithfulness by "dos" and "don'ts") is often a reflection of something quite different from what is taught in the Bible. Jay Kesler, the former president of Youth for Christ and now president of Taylor University, once said that, if the Christian faith were determined by not doing anything wrong, the finest Christian in his household was his dog!

Glenda Sturtevant tells the story of a pastor who was greatly concerned about a new stereo system in one of the social rooms in his church. He was afraid that it would be broken or stolen, so he made a large sign and placed it near the stereo. It read, "This is the eleventh commandment: Thou shalt not touch the stereo system. Signed, The Pastor." A few weeks later, someone wrote on the bottom of the sign: "Thou shalt not make additional commandments. Signed, The Lord."[15]

If you have been a Christian for very long, you know it isn't easy. When one tries to live by what the Bible says, it is a monumental task. What makes it worse is that there are people who want to add to what the Bible says. They want to increase, as it were, the number of commandments. Jesus said, "Woe to you, scribes and Pharisees, hypocrites! For you pay tithe of mint and anise and cumin, and have neglected the weightier matters of the law: justice and mercy and faith" (Matthew 23:23).

Legalism—and the resultant guilt—is one of the great destroyers of boldness and freedom. You will find it in the Christian who is constantly asking if he or she is doing it right or wrong; and who becomes, like the centipede, crippled for want of knowing which foot to put forward. You will find legalism creeping into the life of the new Christian whose joy and freedom are destroyed because some "mature" Christian gave the impression that "real" Christians, in their obedience, have given up everything that was fun, fattening or free. You will find the disease of legalism measuring sin by how much one enjoyed it. (That is, if it was enjoyed, it was a sin. If it was not enjoyed, it was not a sin or, certainly, not a bad one.) Legalism comes from the mouth of Satan, the accuser, who tells the Christian, "If you were really a Christian, you wouldn't act that way." You will find legalism in the pulpit and in the pew as Christians become desperately concerned with their and others' purity and rightness. The question of ultimate concern for the legalist is, "What will others say?" The great commandment for the legalist is, "Thou shalt be like me."

Legalism can kill the necessary freedom of boldness. Let's talk about it.

The Christian Magna Charta

The book of Galatians is an exciting book because it contains some of the most freeing teaching in all the Scripture. We have already looked at some of its teaching. Because of its emphasis on freedom, Galatians has been called "the Magna Charta of Christian liberty." In that book, Paul addressed the Galatians about one of the most priceless gifts of God, freedom.

Some thirteen years from the date of Paul's conversion, Barnabas came to get Paul and enlist his help with the believers in Antioch; God had deemed that it was time for Paul to be used in the service of the King. A lot happened at Antioch, but one of the major happenings was that the believers sent Paul and Barnabas on the first missionary journey of the church.

On that first missionary journey, Paul and Barnabas visited the towns in the southern part of Galatia, a Roman province. They established churches in Pisidia, Antioch, Iconium, Lystra and Derbe.

After the completion of that first journey, Paul and Barnabas returned to Syrian Antioch and told how God had manifested His grace to the people of Galatia. Everyone was excited about what God was doing.

And then the disturbing reports started coming in. They told of how the new Christians in Galatia were turning away from the excitement and freedom of their first love. The reports told of the horror of "legalism" and how it was destroying the joy of the believers. Paul, with the love and firmness of a mother correcting her children, sat down and wrote a letter. The letter he wrote is in your Bible and is known as Galatians. It was probably the earliest letter of Paul that we have in the Bible, and, as such, it reflects the thoughts of Paul in their earliest and, in one sense, clearest form.

In my mind's eye, I can see the great apostle bending over a small writing table using the light of a flickering candle. I can see him pausing often in his writing to think—and sometimes to calm his anger. If you read the book of Galatians, it is possible to think of Paul as an angry, vindictive man. He wrote such things as "But even if we, or an angel from heaven, preach any other gospel to you than what we have preached to you, let him be accursed" (1:8). His imagery was not what one would want to be used in church. As we have already seen, in referring to circumcision he blurts out, "I could wish that those who trouble you would even cut themselves off!" (5:12).

The tone of Galatians is harsh, but it is the harshness that comes from a broken heart. Paul's heart was broken over the destruction taking place among God's people. If you had watched him write and you had looked closely, you would have seen tears falling on the parchment on which Paul penned his letter. In what follows I want to take my cue from Paul's letter to the Galatians in both content and attitude. There is probably nothing in all of Christendom that ticks me off more than unthinking legalism. I believe it has hurt more Christians than we would ever believe. I don't want to be anything less than strong and clear in what I say about it.

On the other hand, I also realize that the disease of legalism is, more often than not, seen in Christians who love Christ the most. Recently, some people in a conference at which I was speaking had been very critical of some other Christians who were taking the gospel to the world in different cultural forms. They were using rock music to proclaim Christ. (Incidentally, you should know that many of the hymns we are now using in our churches were the beer-drinking tunes of the eighteenth century.)

That evening I had decided that I was going to get those "narrow-minded turkeys." But, before I spoke, the Father spoke. He said, "Son, you must remember that these people who make you so angry are the people who love Me the most. They are My flock, and you must not beat them. I didn't call you to beat people, I called you to teach. Do what I told you to do." So let's consider some of the teaching in the book of Galatians: It is the basis for dealing with the problem of guilt in our lives.

Bad News and Very Bad News

Did you hear about the man who went to his doctor and the doctor told him that he had some bad news and some very bad news? The man asked to hear the bad news first, and the doctor said, "The bad news is that I have examined your tests and you have twenty-four hours to live."

"That is really bad news," exclaimed the man. "What in the world could be worse than that?"

"The very bad news is," said the doctor, "I should have talked to you yesterday."

As we talk about the book of Galatians, I have some bad news and some very bad news. But hang on. Before we finish, I also have some very good news for you.

The Bad News

The bad news concerns the law:

For as many as are of the works of the law are under the curse; for it is written, "Cursed is everyone who does not continue in all things which are written in the book of the law, to do them." But that no one is justified by the law in the sight of God is evident, for "The just shall live by faith." Yet the law is not of faith, but "The man who does them shall live by them" (3:10–12). What purpose then does the law serve? It was added because of transgressions (3:19). Is the law then against the promises of God? Certainly not! For if there had been a law given which could have given life, truly righteousness would have been by the law (3:21). Therefore the law was our tutor to bring us to Christ, that we might be justified by faith. But after faith has come, we are no longer under a tutor (3:24–25).

The bad news is that we are under a curse—the curse is the law. Paul said, "For as many as are of the works of the law are under the curse" (3:10). There is something in us that confirms our most horrible fears. There is a righteous and holy God, and His demands are righteous and holy. There is a sense in all of us that somehow we have offended Him and that we will someday have to answer for it.

Silly, old fashioned nonsense.

Right? Wrong. And you know it in your heart.

In fact, I believe that legalism has as its root cause the knowledge that we have to be better than we are lest we offend a holy and righteous God. If going to church is not enough, then honoring the "Lord's day" ought to be added to going to church. If you still feel you don't have it, you decide that what one ought to do is to read the Bible, pray all day Sunday and give up television. And then you still don't feel holy, so you give up television all week, read the Bible and pray a few more hours. If that still doesn't cut it, you fast one day a week. If that doesn't work, you add movies, makeup, dancing, smoking, drinking, novels, card playing and "secular" music to the list of things you ought to give up. And then, if you have done all of that and you still don't feel you please a holy and righteous God, you try to get others to go to church, read the Bible, pray on Sunday, give up television on Sunday, give up television the rest of the week, pray more and read the Bible more, give up movies, makeup, dancing, smoking, drinking, novels, card playing and "secular" music. If they refuse, of course, they have misused their liberty.

Paul called the process the "curse" of the law and it is a real curse. It is the awareness of how much the real God demands and the imposed necessity of trying to meet those demands. That is the bad news.

Very Bad News

The very bad news is that you can't do it. It would be good if we could, because the law is not bad in the sense that what God tells us we ought and ought not to do will be harmful. In fact, just the opposite is true. If we could live by the law perfectly, we would be perfectly happy. God's law is the best way to live. The problem is that we are not good enough to live by it. Note what Paul said about the law: "But that no one is justified by the law in the sight of God is evident" (3:11). The law, whether it is the law of God as expressed in Holy Torah or the law expressed in devout Christians who have heaped laws upon laws to help us be faithful to *the* law, is a curse in the sense that it is a puzzle which can't be completed, a book that can't be read, a road that can't be traveled, a mountain that can't be climbed and a task that can't be done.

A friend of mine once posed a riddle to me. He said, "What is yellow, has feathers, sings, plays baseball, and lives in a cage?" I thought for a long time. He said, "Give up?"

I said, "I can't imagine the answer to your riddle. I give up. What is it?"

"A canary."

"A canary?" I sputtered, "A canary doesn't play baseball!"

"Oh," he said, laughing, "I lied about the baseball!"

The law and the laws we make up to keep the law are like that. There are all kinds of promises. If you just work hard enough at it, if you add to your list of "don'ts" and subtract from your list of "dos," eventually you will be clean, pure, honest, sweet, kind, loving, obedient and faithful. Then, God will notice how good you are doing and how hard you are trying, and He will love you.

And then we try—we really try. At the end of our trying, we know we have failed. And the law says, "I lied about the success."

I have a friend who decided that he would not work or cause anyone else to work on the Lord's day. So he stopped taking the Sunday paper because he didn't want to cause the paperboy or the reporters to work on Sunday. He stopped taking the bus to church because he didn't want the bus driver to work on Sunday, and he quit going to restaurants on Sunday so he wouldn't make those folks work.

To help him see the futility of this approach, I asked if he used electricity in his house on Sunday. He agreed that he did, and I reminded him that he was causing the people at the power company to work on Sunday. I told him that a lot of the features used in the newspaper on Sunday were written during the week. Not only that, I said, but the Sunday paper is printed on Saturday, so if he really wanted to be consistent he would have to stop taking the Monday paper. In fact, he would have to stop taking the paper altogether, because, by buying the paper he contributed to the institution that supported the reporters who wrote during the week for the Sunday paper and, thereby, caused others to work on Sunday. I suggested that he ought to give up the bus all the time. After all, the mechanics had to work on Sunday to make sure the bus would run on Monday. "The restaurants," I went on, "have to prepare a lot of their food on Saturday—"

"Wait a minute," he said, "I get your point. I give up."

My friend was beginning to see the very bad news. All of us have seen the very bad news whenever we have tried to live up to God's standard as given to us in the Bible, or to man's standard as given to us by the legalists. We want to cry out with Paul, "O wretched man that I am! Who will deliver me from this body of death?" (Romans 7:24).

Dear friend, you can't live up to the standards. I know how hard you have been working at it. I know all you have given up—all the pain and hurt. I know the people who have called you a fanatic and the pagans who have made fun of you. I know the times when you have denied yourself, when you have turned away from worldliness. I know the tears you have shed and the times you have asked forgiveness and promised to be better, only to find yourself back in the same old trap. I know the number of times you have gone over the "check list" to make sure you didn't miss anything, and the horror you felt when you discovered that you had. I know the sleepless nights and the dull, unhappy days. I also know you did it for God. The very bad news is that all your efforts are for nothing. You have been reaching for a golden ring . . . and the golden ring is just an illusion.

The Good News

I promised to give you the bad news and the very bad news, and I have. But, I also promised to give you the very good news. Paul called the law a curse, but he also suggested it is a blessed curse:

> Is the law then against the promises of God? Certainly not! For if there had been a law given which could have given life, truly righteousness would have been by the law . . . Therefore the law was our tutor to bring us to Christ. (Galatians 3:21, 24)

Author Frederick Buechner described how his mother and brother dealt with his father's suicide. They moved to Bermuda. His grandmother was a harsh and, in some ways, wise woman who had learned from her father that the best way to deal with the harshness of life was to stare it right in the eye and face it down. "She was right that reality can be harsh and that you shut your eyes to it only at your peril because if you do not face up to the enemy in all of his dark power, then the enemy will come up from behind some dark day and destroy you while you are facing the other way."[16]

Buechner's grandmother told the family to stay in New York and face reality. But Buechner pointed out something that runs through the very core of the universe. He wrote:

> To do for yourself the best that you have it in you to do—to grit your teeth and clench your fists in order to survive the world at its harshest and worst—is, by that very act, to be unable to let something be done for you and in you that is more wonderful still. The trouble with steeling yourself against the harshness of reality is that the same steel that secures your life against being destroyed secures your life also against being opened up and transformed by the holy power that life itself comes from.[17]

What Buechner said about standing against reality without giving in can be said about the way we deal with the law and the laws. When you can't do any more, you discover something wonderful. Jesus Christ has done it for you. Paul said, "Christ has redeemed us from the curse of the law, having become a curse for us" (Galatians 3:13).

C. S. Lewis had a great comment on those who try to live by the law. He said that, one way or the other, one of two results will follow:

> Either we give up trying to be good, or else we become very unhappy indeed. For, make no mistake: If you are really going to try to meet all the demands made on the natural self, it will not have enough left over to live on. The more you obey your conscience, the more your conscience will demand of you. And your natural self, which is thus being starved and hampered and worried at every turn, will get angrier and angrier. In the end, you will either give up trying to be good, or else become one of those people who, as they say, "live for others" but always in a discontented, grumbling way—always making a martyr of yourself. And once you have become that you will be a far greater pest to anyone who has to live with you than you would have been if you had remained frankly selfish.[18]

So, what do you do? Let me tell you. Give everything you have to Christ. Accept His acceptance. Give up the battle and begin to live. He has promised to give you His Spirit. That is a reality you don't have to think about all the time any more than you have to think about how to ride a bicycle when you're on it. You simply ride the bicycle.

The Christian lives a life of faith. Faith in what? Faith in the promise of Christ that you are accepted, not on the basis of how good you are, but on the basis of how good He is. Every once in a while, you need to check the law of the Bible because it reflects God's will. When Jesus said that He had not come to destroy the law but to fulfill it, He meant that He had come to give His people the power to live by God's law (still the best way to live) and forgiveness when they didn't. The law (not the laws we create) is a good measurement. He wants you to check it, *not so you can see how bad you are doing, but so you can see how well you are doing by His grace.*

The famous statement of Augustine's about loving God and doing as you please is true. When you love Him, that is all you have to do. In a response to His love, give Him yourself—everything. His love will hold you and mold you and change you. Paul put it this way:

> I have been crucified with Christ; it is no longer I who live, but Christ lives in me; and the life which I now live in the flesh I live by faith in the Son of God, who loved me and gave Himself for me. (Galatians 2:20)

Now you can be free to be bold.

My friend, Jim Green, told me about an interesting incident that happened on the first live nationwide television broadcast. Because it was a first, a number of prominent people were asked to address the nation. Conrad Hilton was among those who had that opportunity. Everyone waited to see what this great man would say to such a tremendous audience. He said, "A number of you have stayed at Hilton hotels. Let me ask you to do something for me. When you take a shower, make sure the shower curtain is on the inside of the tub."

Can you believe that? What a great opportunity . . . and he talks about shower curtains! It reminds me of those folks who take the precious gift of freedom and joy given to the Christian and who make a mockery of it by destroying it with rules and regulations.

Do you know what God would have said given the same setting? He would have said, "A number of you have stayed at Hilton hotels. I'm glad. I want you to enjoy it and to have a good time. If you have a problem, just let me know about it."

Of course, the Christian life is not a Hilton hotel. It is a lot more serious than that. However, God does own the hotel and He makes the rules. Just make sure that they are His rules you are following and not those of one of the bellboys. His rules are not all that tough. In fact, there is only one. He wants you to die, so He can live through you. Once He begins to live through you, you own the hotel too.

Keep that in mind as we now expose the problem of guilt. When you become imprisoned by legalism and find yourself unable to live by the good news of freedom and boldness in Christ, then you open yourself up to unnecessary guilt.

I live in a rather affluent area of the country. Sometimes when I see all that I have, I feel guilty. I have noticed that the more I acquire, the more time I must expend to protect all my acquisitions. In other words, I have lots of stuff, and I am getting to the point of spending much of my time protecting my stuff. Don't be so shocked. The Father is dealing with me (Hurricane Andrew, for example!) and I am learning, by His grace, to work toward simplicity in my life. I know all the things Jesus said about the rich and I also know the dangers of modern-day materialism.

The point is that, when you have much, you feel compassion for those who have little. And it is a very small step from compassion to guilt. One of the most interesting phenomena of our time is the "political left" bias of the wealthy. The spectrum runs from the wealthy suburbanite who has a plan to distribute everybody else's wealth, to the "radical chic" of New York and Los Angeles, to the daughter of wealthy parents who, feeling guilty for the wealth in which she has grown up, becomes an expert on making bombs to kill the bourgeoisie.

Please understand that I am not making a political statement. That isn't the issue here. Because Hitler believed the multiplication tables does not make the multiplication tables wrong. The point is that a lot of the political left, when seen among the wealthy, is the result of guilt and not the result of rational process of thought.

A number of years ago, Rusty Anderson, a stockbroker friend of mine, and I decided that we needed to minister to the poor. We prayed about it and decided that, when we ministered to the poor, we shouldn't be in the position of a leader. What we needed to do was to really get down and do some manual labor—to, as it were, "get our hands dirty" with and for the poor.

Rusty had a friend who was a Salvation Army officer. So, he asked his friend if there were something we could do to help him out. The Salvation Army officer was surprised, but he accepted our offer to do some work around the Salvation Army. After all, it wasn't often that a stockbroker and a Presbyterian pastor made that kind of offer.

Early one Saturday morning, Rusty and I, dressed in our dirty jeans and old shirts, made our way to "minister to the poor." When I picked Rusty up that morning, he told me he didn't know exactly where we were going, but that he was sure it was down in the slums. So, we headed for the ghetto and checked the address, only to discover that it was not right in the ghetto, but farther out. We got on the right street and started counting numbers. The closer we got to the right number, the better the neighborhood looked. In fact, we started going by some places that made us look poor.

By the time we got to the Salvation Army church, we were in the suburbs and (I suspect that this is the exception for most Salvation Army works) it was a magnificent building with landscaped grounds more beautiful than the buildings and grounds of some of the wealthiest churches in Miami.

But we had promised, so we reported to Rusty's friend and began to work. I was given a lawn mower, and Rusty some hedge clippers. Every time I pushed my lawn mower past Rusty, who was clipping the hedge, we would break out in gales of laughter. How silly we looked! What idiots we had made of ourselves in our efforts to "help the poor."

Rusty and I have laughed about that incident a number of times over the years. We are a little bit wiser now and a lot older. One of the things we have come to realize is that there is great motivating power in guilt. Let's talk about it.

Guilt As a Motivator

A number of years ago, a study was done on people who had entered "full-time" Christian service. The object of the study was to determine the psychological motives for entering a religious profession. The results were interesting. The study revealed that a great majority of people who serve in full-time religious jobs were there because of guilt. In other words, guilt was the motivating factor.

I suspect that, if we were to do a similar study on laymen and laywomen in the church, we would find that there, too, one of the significant motivating factors in their decision to be in the church was a high degree of guilt.

Don't get me wrong. I believe we are guilty. The Bible teaches:

For when we were still without strength, in due time Christ died for the ungodly. For scarcely for a righteous man will one die; yet perhaps for a good man someone would even dare to die. But God demonstrates His own love toward us, in that while we were still sinners, Christ died for us. (Romans 5:6–8)

Jeremiah 17:9 says:

The heart is deceitful above all things, and desperately wicked; Who can know it?

I used to believe that there were two kinds of people in the world: the good and the bad. The bad people drank too much, cursed too much, smoked too much and mowed their lawns on Sunday. The good people did not drink too much, curse too much or smoke too much, and they went to church on Sunday. I was not a pastor for very long before I found out that there are indeed two kinds of people in the world: There are bad people who know it and bad people who don't know it. The bad people who know it and want to do something about it are in the church. The bad people who think they are good have no use for Christ or for His church.

Jesus said,

> Those who are well have no need of a physician, but those who are
> sick . . . For I did not come to call the righteous, but sinners, to repen-
> tance. (Matthew 9:12–13)

In other words, if you are following Christ, you do so because
you are a sinner, not because you aren't. The church is a fellowship of people who have been forgiven and are in the process of
change.

Thus, it is only natural that one would find Christians who are
aware of their sin in the church and in positions of leadership of
the church. Guilt is certainly a proper factor in people's coming to
Christ—maybe the only legitimate one. The essence of the Christian faith is a paradox. In order to qualify for it, first you have to
admit you're unqualified for it.

But, in this chapter, I'm not talking about forgiven sinners; I'm
talking about forgiven sinners who either don't "feel" forgiven or
who act as if they aren't forgiven. If you fall into that category, you
are vulnerable to every religious huckster and con man who comes
down the pike. It is open season on guilt-ridden Christians . . . and
that makes me angry. It makes me angry at the religious hucksters
and con men who use guilt to motivate. Not only that, it also makes
me angry when I or other people in my family allow ourselves to
be manipulated by guilt.

How Guilt Works

If we are going to talk about guilt, it would be good to find out
what it is. *The Psychiatric Dictionary* (4th edition) gives the following definition:

> Realization that one has done wrong by violating some ethical,
> moral or religious principle. Associated with such realization typ-
> ically are lowered self-esteem and a feeling that one should expi-
> ate or make retribution for the wrong that has been done.

As used in psychoanalytic writings, the term usually refers to neurotic, unreasonable, or pathologic guilt feelings that do not appear to be justified by the reasons adduced for the guilt.

Now, in order to understand how guilt works, let me give you a highly simplified four-step description of the *healthy* way to deal with guilt. First, there is the violation of a standard. That standard can be a biblical standard, a personal moral code or a code one has accepted from one's peers. Whatever the standard, there is a real violation that begins the movement toward guilt. For instance, a little girl gets dressed in a new dress. Her mother says to her, "Now honey, you be careful and keep the dress clean." Then suppose the little girl promptly goes out and gets mud on the new dress. She knows that she has violated her mother's standard.

Second, there is the legitimate feeling of guilt. That feeling is the unease we feel when we know something is wrong, that we have fallen short, that we have missed the mark. One of the most dangerous practices in which some people engage is the practice of denying the legitimate feeling of guilt. When I have violated God's standards (or, for that matter, my own best standards), I ought to feel guilty. Unless I accurately identify what the feeling of unease is, I will not be able to do anything about alleviating the unease. A sense of guilt in the face of the violation of legitimate standards is legitimate guilt. To continue the illustration, the little girl says, "I should not have been playing in the mud, but I did and now my dress is dirty. I feel bad about my dress getting dirty."

Third, there is the need for punishment, forgiveness or retribution. One of the great mistakes we have made in our penal system is the one-sided emphasis on rehabilitation. It would be far healthier psychologically if we balanced punishment with rehabilitation. Prison ought to be seen as paying the price or balancing the books. The little girl shows her dress to her mother; and, then, her mother either spanks her or forgives her.

Finally, there is the freedom from guilt. After one has done something wrong, felt guilty about it and received punishment, forgiveness or retribution, one is then free of the guilt. Our little girl, after her spanking, is a very happy little girl because she doesn't feel bad about herself. She has paid the price. Now, she can go on about her business until the next time (and there *will* be a next time) she gets her dress dirty.

What I've described above is a perfectly healthy way to deal with guilt. We have all used that system, even without knowing it, to deal with our own guilt. For Christians, the third step was the action of Christ. He died for our sins; and, as a result, we have forgiveness and freedom.

Illegitimate Guilt

The problem comes when the first step is not an actual violation of a definable standard. In other words, if we feel guilty when we are not objectively guilty, the system doesn't work. What one does when there has been no legitimate violation, yet still feelings of guilt, is to go back and forth between steps two and three without ever feeling free.

Let me illustrate what I mean. A number of years ago, I spent considerable time counseling Sally, a young woman who had become a prostitute. She didn't like herself and she didn't like her profession; but, after repeated attempts to change, she told me that it was no use. She gave up.

Let me tell you Sally's story. When Sally was a year old, her mother had a lobotomy (i.e., a psychosurgical procedure). The surgery left her mother without the ability to function, so she was placed in an institution for custodial care for the rest of her life. Sally's father, knowing there was no way he could work and take care of his daughter, placed Sally with two maiden aunts.

A one-year-old child doesn't have the ability to reason. But my friend could feel and her feelings were, "I used to have a mother who loved me. She left me. My father loved me too and he got rid of me. There must be something very wrong with me." In other words, Sally had significant feelings of guilt, yet she had not violated any standard.

I talked to another young girl whose mother was raped. The girl I counseled had absolutely nothing to do with the situation. She was asleep in her room when the incident happened. When I first talked to her, however, she was quick to assert that she had opened the door to the rapist. Somehow, because the incident was understandably traumatic to the mother and caused the mother to turn in on herself, my friend began to think, *I must have had something to do with the rape.* It was a short step from that feeling to the belief that she had actually opened the door to the rapist when she had not.

There was also the teenager whose father was killed in an automobile accident. The father and son relationship was rather strained, as is often the case during a son's adolescence. When I talked to the young man, he told me he was responsible for his father's accident. He wasn't, but he had feelings of guilt.

There was the father who told me, after his wife died, that he had trouble dealing with the guilt he felt. I asked him why he felt guilty, and he told me he didn't know why, but he did.

When my own parents would have an argument during my childhood, I used to wonder what was wrong with me. Of course, nothing was wrong with me. I wasn't the one doing the arguing, but I still felt guilty. People are my business; over and over again I have encountered Christians who feel guilty without having violated any standard.

When the feelings of guilt are not related to the reality of violation, one still tries to resolve the guilt in a healthy way (i.e., punishment, forgiveness or retribution). Because there is no legitimate violation, though, there is never freedom. One simply feels more and more guilty, trying to resolve the greater guilt with the same method. In other words, we set up situations in which we are punished; we are constantly seeking forgiveness and forever trying to "balance the books."

- Are you constantly "putting yourself down?"
- Do you sometimes say to yourself, "I'm just a klutz. I never do anything right"?
- Do you spend much of your time apologizing to other people?
- Have you confessed a particular sin to God a thousand times, wondering when He is going to forgive you?
- Do you constantly find yourself in a predicament where you get hurt?
- Are you always afraid to confront other people with a difficult truth?
- When you are accused of something, do you always assume you are at fault?
- Do you always dread disagreements?
- Are you always defending yourself against some real or imagined wrong?
- When a clerk in a department store is rude to you, do you wonder what you did wrong?
- Whenever your pastor preaches on almost any sin, do you find yourself blushing?
- When you read the Bible, do you find yourself always underlining the passages that deal with sin and failure?
- Do you sometimes get to the edge of success and then do something stupid to ruin it?
- Do you find yourself embarrassed by compliments and ill at ease when others praise you?

If you have answered any of the above questions in the affirmative, it is likely that you have a problem with illegitimate guilt. (If you answered none of the above questions in the affirmative, then you will probably lie about other things too!) As a matter of fact, we all carry some emotional baggage around. Because that is true, we are vulnerable to the manipulation of guilt to the degree in which we suffer from illegitimate guilt.

How to Handle Illegitimate Guilt

The question that immediately comes to mind is this: What do I do about it? Unfortunately, there is no system in which you can just go through the right steps and are thereby freed from illegitimate guilt. It is a lifelong struggle for many of us. However, there are some guidelines that can help.

Understand the Standard

First, you can make sure you understand the standard. In other words, you can be aware of the standard by which you measure yourself and understand the specifics of that standard. Because I am a Christian, the Bible is my standard. It is my responsibility to know what the Bible says in regard to how I act, think, work and believe. I know that the Bible tells me I ought to be truthful. When I am not truthful, because I know what the standard is, I feel guilty. At that point, I ought to be guilty because I have violated my standard.

A man who has a reputation for being a Christian once called me and asked if he could have a few minutes of my time. He said he was dealing with a difficult problem and needed some help. When the man came into my study, he wasted no time in getting down to the problem.

He said, "Pastor, I don't want to waste your time or mine. I am trying to determine what God would have me do about my mistress."

I asked him, "You mean that you are trying to find enough emotional power to say 'no' to that particular sin?"

"No," he said, "I am trying to act in a loving way. I love my wife and I love my mistress, and I want to do the Christian thing."

I asked the man if he believed the Bible and wanted to govern his life accordingly. He replied that, of course, he believed the Bible because he was a Christian.

Yet, his standard was not the Bible. When I took him to a number of biblical texts that dealt with his specific actions, he rejected what the Bible had to say. He said that his standard was the Bible; but, the fact is, his real standard was either self-gratification or some kind of nebulous definition of love. He had not clearly decided on his standard.

We often say that we accept the Bible as our standard when, in reality, our standard is the approval of our peers, the pleasure of our mother or the accumulation of wealth. It is important that, as Christians, we understand that our only legitimate standard is the Bible. Then, when we violate that standard, we can deal with the violation in a healthy way.

Face the Reality of the Fall

Second, in order to deal with illegitimate guilt, you need to face the reality of the Fall. In other words, one needs to recognize that perfection is impossible in government, in education, in the church and in one's heart. Political statism (i.e., the view that advocates heavy involvement of the state in the control, especially economic, of the country) is a fallacy because it is based on the untruth that government is perfectible. Perfectionism in the church creates more guilt than sin and can destroy Christians. I have a Catholic priest friend who has a card he sometimes gives people. On one side is written, "Bless those who curse you . . . " On the other side, " . . . because they may be right."

I have written in the back of my Bible, "You wouldn't be so shocked at your own sin if you didn't have such a high opinion of yourself." I sometimes flip to the back of my Bible and read that just before I preach. It helps me deal with my real sins and also the vague feeling of guilt that I can't attach to any biblical standard I have violated.

An old, wise statement makes the point well: "There is so much bad in the best of us and so much good in the worst of us that it ill behooves any of us to judge the rest of us." That philosophy ought to be applied to oneself as well.

Please understand, though, that I'm not excusing sin. I am, rather, defining reality. When one experiences feelings of illegitimate guilt, one ought to be able to say to oneself, "Of course I feel guilty. Some of it is deserved, but I have been forgiven and am getting better. Other times, I feel guilty when I ought not to feel guilty. I'm also forgiven for feeling guilty when I ought not to feel guilty. Therefore, I don't have to feel guilty."

Discover the Sources

Third, it is important that you discover the sources of illegitimate guilt. Ask the Father why you feel so inferior to other people, why you always assume you are wrong, why you are afraid to confront and why you care so much what people think about you. Then, be silent before the Father, allowing Him to draw up the memories so that He can heal. Perhaps you need, if it is a major problem, to talk to your pastor or a wise friend. An alcoholic parent, a traumatic sexual experience, a cruel comment made to you when you were a child, an overemphasis on perfection, or a recurring physical sickness are just a few of the areas in which we can begin to develop feelings of guilt that are not related to reality. Allow the Father to bring them to memory. Then, begin to deal with them by asking Him to take the memories He shows you. One of the interesting aspects about debilitating memories is that they die (or almost die) in the light.

Appreciate God's Grace

Fourth, in dealing with illegitimate guilt, you must have a high (i.e., biblical) view of God's grace. Too many Christians speak biblical doctrine with their mouths and, yet, live the American folk religion with their lives. The Bible says:

> For by grace you have been saved through faith, and that not of yourselves; it is the gift of God. (Ephesians 2:8)

In Romans 5:20 Paul writes:

But where sin abounded, grace abounded much more.

Someone tells the story about the man who went to heaven and was, thereupon, confronted by Peter, who said to the man, "In order to get into heaven you must have one thousand points. What have you done to earn your one thousand points?"

The man said, "I never heard that before, but I'm sure I have earned at least that many. I am the father of three children, and I have been a good father and husband. I have never cheated on my wife or mistreated my children. One of my boys is a pastor, another a missionary, and my daughter is a nurse, working in the slums of our city. I am a banker and I give over 20 percent of my income to the Lord's work. But I don't just give money, I put my life and my words where my money is. In my bank, I have worked to bring low income housing to the poor in my city. I spend one night a week working in a clinic in the slums. I have put a number of poor kids through college and I support a number of missionaries on the field. Every Christmas, I go with the Salvation Army in our city to help them raise money. I always support my pastor and his work for the Lord, and I have been an elder in our church almost all of my adult life. Most of my deeds are done in secret and I have built, anonymously, an educational wing of our church and a hospital in Haiti."

The man looked over to Peter and asked, "How am I doing?"

Peter replied, "Well, that's one point. Have you done anything else?"

"Good night!" the man exclaimed, "God have mercy!"

Peter laughed and said, "You've got it! That's a thousand points. Come on in."

Sometimes, it is good to deeply reflect on the grace of God. His grace is absolutely sufficient. He has done everything necessary to make us acceptable . . . and we *are* therefore acceptable.

Paul Tournier, in his old but good book, *Guilt and Grace*, has made the point that true guilt and false (i.e., illegitimate) guilt can be separated by knowing that true guilt is a violation of God's standards and false guilt violates man's standards. He then goes on to make a very profound statement:

> Therefore, real guilt is often something quite different from that which constantly weighs us down, because of our fear of social judgment and the disapproval of men. We become independent of them in proportion as we depend on God.[19]

The more we concentrate on the grace of God and the less we concentrate on ourselves, the freer we become.

Act Forgiven

Finally, in dealing with illegitimate guilt, you need to learn to follow the advice given to John Wesley, "Fake it till you make it." (Well, that isn't exactly the advice he was given, but it's close.) Wesley was once in great difficulty because he didn't believe in the concept of faith. He went to his spiritual advisor, who said, "Wesley, preach faith until you have faith, and then, because you have faith, you will preach faith." In other words, Wesley was asked to fake it until he made it.

Now, lest you accuse me of advocating hypocrisy, let me suggest that I am not advocating hypocrisy; but, rather, obedience. If you were free from debilitating guilt, if you thought you had been made worthy by the blood of Christ, if you knew you were free of feelings of unworthiness, what would you do? *Do it.* Why? Because, if you are a Christian, you are, in fact, worthy and free from guilt. By conforming to a reality instead of to a lie, you will come to reflect in your feelings, as well as your life, the reality of a forgiven sinner who is clean.

The Christian who is manipulated by guilt (either legitimate or illegitimate) is denying the very reality of his or her life. Please don't allow the death of Christ to be wasted.

Evangelist Leighton Ford told about a man who owned a Rolls Royce. While traveling on vacation, there was a mechanical failure. The man called the company from which he had bought the car and they flew in a mechanic from England to repair it. After waiting a number of weeks for a bill for the repair job, the man wrote to the company in England and asked for a bill. He received a telex. It read: "We have no record of a Rolls Royce with a mechanical failure."

Because of the death of Christ, the Christian stands free, clean and bold before the God of the universe. An understanding of that fact is absolutely necessary if any Christian is going to stand against the pagan and religious manipulation of our time. When we who trust in the atoning work of Christ go before the judgment seat of God, He will say, "I have no record of the failure."

6

Problem #2

Fear, the Bane of Boldness

The second problem which stands in the way of our becoming free and bold, as Christians, is the problem of fear, the bane of boldness.

Jean Shepherd, in a humorous and insightful article, "The Decline and Fall of the Wimp," wrote:

> Scholars studying the field (*Wimpus apologeticus americanus*) believe the high point of wimpishness was captured by a photographer showing President Jimmy Carter seated in a rowboat fighting off an attacking killer rabbit with an oar. From that moment on, wimps were in retreat, casting nervous glances behind them in fear of pursuing rabbits, while the rest of us instinctively sighed in relief, hoping that the whole madness was now exposed and would die of its own nervousness. As my Aunt Clara used to say: "My best friend, Mabel, died of nerves." I never knew what she meant, but I do now.[20]

While guilt may be the greatest motivating factor in the creation of the wimp (Shepherd says that if a plague of locusts descends on an obscure country 12,000 miles away, a wimp will ask, "How have I failed them? Where did I go wrong?"), fear and worry run a very close second. In the parable of the talents, Jesus told us about three different reactions to the master who gave different talents to his servants while he, the master, went away. The first and the second servants went out and increased the master's money, but the third hid what the master had given him in the ground. When

121

asked why he didn't at least invest the money and get the interest for the master, the servant replied, "I knew you to be a hard man, reaping where you have not sown, and gathering where you have not scattered seed. *And I was afraid"* (Matthew 25:24–25, italics mine).

Fear is the bane of boldness. "I was afraid." Those words have accounted for more failure to stand where God would have the Christian stand than almost anything else. It isn't that we don't know where to stand; it isn't that we don't want to stand. The problem is—we're afraid. We're afraid we might fail; we're afraid people may not like us; we're afraid that we might get out of the will of God; we're afraid of the wrath of God; we're afraid of what people will do to us if they get angry; we're afraid of cancer, pollution, war and AIDS. We're afraid not to be afraid, lest, in our moment of weakness, we get destroyed. We're afraid of losing our material goods and our spiritual superiority. We're afraid, with Satchel Paige, to look back lest something should be gaining on us. And, most of all, we're afraid of death.

Jake Fen, a Hungarian, had a funny sense of humor. One time, he came upon the novel idea to end his wife's incessant nagging by letting her know how she would feel if he committed suicide. So, Mr. Fen built an elaborate harness to make it appear as though he had hung himself. His unsuspecting wife came in from shopping, saw her husband hanging from the rafter, let out a scream and promptly fainted.

A neighbor, hearing the scream, came over. Finding what she logically assumed were two corpses, she took the opportunity to loot the apartment. As the neighbor was leaving, her arms laden with loot, the outraged and very alive Mr. Fen kicked her stoutly in the backside. The neighbor, knowing that dead folks don't kick that hard, promptly died of a heart attack. Mr. Fen was acquitted of manslaughter; and, at last report, Mrs. Fen was trying to forgive him.[21]

Fear can kill you; but, even more important than that, fear can kill your boldness and freedom. Unless the believer can find a healthy way to deal with fear, boldness is not an option. Let's talk about it.

First, I want you to remember that fear is not, in itself, a bad thing. In fact, fear, like pain, can be God's way of turning on the warning system. Paul Brand and Philip Yancey, in their fine book, *In His Image*, point out that leprosy is not a disease that simply causes deterioration. It also causes the loss of feeling. Often, the deterioration is not because of the disease itself; but because, without pain, people do things they wouldn't ordinarily do, such as placing a hand on a hot stove, gripping a saw in the wrong place or holding a doorknob too tightly. They comment, "Leprosy patients suffer because they feel no pain; they yearn for the demons who would alert them to impending danger."[22]

Just as pain is a gift from God to warn us of a problem, so fear can be a gift from God to enable us to stay out of trouble or, when we are in trouble, to "stir up the juices" in our bodies so we can act appropriately. That great "theologian" Fran Tarkenton once said, "Fear causes people to draw back from situations; it brings on mediocrity; it dulls creativity; it sets one up to be a loser in life." That, of course, is true, but it is important to see the other side of the picture. Fear causes people to draw back from dangerous situations; it brings on mediocrity, but it also challenges us to greatness; it dulls creativity, but it also produces it; it sets one up to be a loser in life, but it also makes for winners. Fran Tarkenton would be the first to admit that, without fear, his record-setting football career would have been something less than it was.

Someone tells the story about the two men who were out walking in the woods when they heard the roar of a grizzly bear. Both men were frightened . . . and with reason. One man promptly sat down and started putting on his running shoes. The other said to him, "Jim, you don't think you're going to outrun that bear, do you?"

Jim replied, "Of course I'm not going to outrun that bear. I don't have to. I just have to outrun you."

Using Fear to Your Advantage

Fear is sometimes a great and good motivator. The question then is: How can I use fear to my advantage?

Let's turn to an incident in the incarnational life of Jesus for some answers. In Mark 4, Jesus was tired and trying to get a little rest by moving away from the multitude. Mark wrote:

> On the same day, when evening had come, He said to them, "Let us cross over to the other side." Now when they had left the multitude, they took Him along in the boat as He was. And other little boats were also with Him. And a great windstorm arose, and the waves beat into the boat, so that it was already filling. But He was in the stern, asleep on a pillow. And they awoke Him and said to Him, "Teacher, do You not care that we are perishing?" Then He arose and rebuked the wind, and said to the sea, "Peace, be still!" And the wind ceased and there was a great calm. But He said to them, "Why are you so fearful? How is it that you have no faith?" And they feared exceedingly, and said to one another, "Who can this be, that even the wind and the sea obey Him!" (Mark 4:35–41)

There are a number of items in that text which are relevant to our discussion. First, you need to note that the disciples were afraid . . . and with good reason. At the Sea of Galilee, there are air currents that cause the wind to sweep down the narrow ravines, descending to the shore from the surrounding hills. Those wind storms come with tremendous force and violence. The storms come up literally "out of the blue," and many sailors have died in them.

George Bowman told about a group of university students from Toronto who went up to Georgian Bay for a fishing trip. They hired a boat and a captain to take them out. When they were out on the water, a tremendous storm arose and the captain sat at the helm with a worried look on his face. The students made fun of him. One of the students said, "We aren't afraid. Why should you be afraid?"

The captain looked at them and said, "Yes, you are too ignorant to be afraid."

Well, the disciples of Jesus were not too ignorant to be afraid. They had seen the storms on the Sea of Galilee; after all, they were fishermen. They knew when to be afraid—and this was a time to be afraid.

In his first inaugural address, on March 4, 1933, Franklin Delano Roosevelt said that the only thing we had to fear was fear itself. That sounded nice; it was good rhetoric; it had a nice ring. The problem is that it wasn't true then and it isn't true now. We have a lot to fear and there is something warped about the person who never experiences fear.

One of the most dangerous thoughts a Christian can have is to think a bold, free Christian has no fear. Not only that, but then to actually deny the reality of that fear as well.

I visit a lot of hospitals. I will often ask a person who is facing surgery, "Are you frightened?" I get a great variety of answers to that question. Some Christians say, "No, Pastor, I'm not afraid. Christ is with me, and He has taken the fear." Others will say, "How can I be afraid? I'm a Christian."

Not too long ago, I was visiting a delightful lady and I asked her that question. Her answer was disarming in its honesty. She said, "Don't be silly! Of course, I'm afraid. Do you think I'm a nut? People die in this place. So, you pray for me." That was refreshing!

There is nothing Christian about the denial of reality. The courage of the Christian doesn't come without fear. When you don't have any fear, you don't need any courage. Courage can only be defined in the context of fear. If you never know fear, you will never know courage. The bold, free Christian ought to be the most realistic of people. Others live fairy tales, but not Christians. Pollyanna is another name for pagan. It ought to be quite different for Christians.

The Disciples' Mistakes

The disciples were afraid. In fact, they had every reason to be afraid; their fear was real and legitimate. However, they made some mistakes. We make them too.

Failure to Note the Peace of Jesus

First, the disciples made the mistake of failing to note the peace of Jesus.

> And a great windstorm arose, and the waves beat into the boat, so that it was already filling. But He was in the stern, asleep on a pillow. (vv. 37–38)

As I mentioned before, I have a friend who is a pilot. While I'm afraid of flying, I don't mind flying with my friend. Do you know why? Because I can watch my friend's face. When he starts perspiring, I know it's time for me to commence praying. If he's calm, I'm calm. And, if he's frightened, I'm frightened. In other words, I get my cue from the pilot, who knows when it is time to be afraid. If he isn't afraid, I figure I don't have to be either.

If I had been on the boat with Jesus, I believe I would have watched Him. I probably would have made several trips to the stern of the boat, and each time I would have checked on Jesus. As long as He was asleep, I could control my fear. If Jesus had awakened, however, I would have gone into a panic.

There was a couple in the church I once served who were threatened with death if they didn't give in to certain demands. They stood their ground, but sometimes it was scary. The wife was remarkably calm during the whole experience, though. I called them once, after one particularly harsh threat, and talked to her. She said. "Pastor, up until now, I have been okay. But Ron was a little frightened tonight. When he gets frightened, I know it is time for me to be frightened."

Let me tell you something: When Jesus gets frightened, I know it is time to be frightened. But so far, when I have gone to Him, He has never been frightened.

Thomas Kelly talked about a calm altar in our heart where we can go to worship at any time. He said that, no matter what is going on outside, we can go to that altar. What I am advocating is that we spend more time at the altar. Please understand that I am not giving the banal advice that, if you are afraid, pray about it. What I am saying is that there is a calm place before the throne of Christ. We ought to spend more time there, because we will always leave the calmness of His presence more calm than when we went in.

Most of my Christian life, I have been a Christian simply because the Christian faith is true. I had determined intellectually that it was true; and if it was true, then, insofar as possible, I would live out its implications. That sounds good; but, after a few years, it gets sort of old. Understand that I am not talking about salvation. I was saved; I simply knew it more in my mind than I felt it in my heart.

A few years ago, I prayed a life-changing prayer. I said: "Father, you know that I know a lot about you. I have a big library, I study the Bible and I know theology. You also know that I'm never going to leave. No matter what happens, I am still going to keep on trucking. But, Father, I want to do more than just know *about* you. I want to know you. I want to experience your presence in the way that a lot of my brothers and sisters experience it. I want the experience as well as the knowledge. Whatever it takes, allow me to know you the way they do."

I won't try to tell you that I have since become a spiritual giant. I haven't. I don't even know enough to talk much about it. And I certainly haven't experienced it enough to teach about it. But, since then, I have discovered God in a very significant and different way from the way I had known Him before. Here is the point: I met God on the other side of silence. In the quiet, sometimes He comes. When my heart is still and waiting, sometimes I am able to hear the "soft sound of sandaled feet." Sometimes (not all the time) I can grow quiet and I am in His presence. On those occasions, my fear is less, my heart is calmer and my courage is greater. In fact, even the thought of those times calms my fears.

Failure to Note the Presence of Jesus

The disciples made another mistake. They failed to note the presence of Jesus. Paul wrote to the Romans:

> Who shall separate us from the love of Christ? Shall tribulation, or distress, or persecution, or famine, or nakedness, or peril, or sword? As it is written: "For Your sake we are killed all day long; We are accounted as sheep for the slaughter." Yet in all these things we are more than conquerors through Him who loved us. For I am persuaded that neither death nor life, nor angels nor principalities nor powers, nor things present nor things to come, nor height nor depth, nor any other created thing, shall be able to separate us from the love of God which is in Christ Jesus our Lord. (Romans 8:35–39)

Now that is a wonderful statement! It means that, no matter what happens, a believer is never separated from Christ.

Chuck Colson tells how Henry Kissinger disliked flying—except when Richard Nixon was on the airplane. When the President of the United States was on the plane, Kissinger was calm. Well, I'm not sure that would make me calm, but I'll tell you what does: The fact that Christ is present in my life. That means I don't have to face any difficulty or any fear by myself.

Failure to Note the Power of Jesus

That brings me to the third mistake the disciples made. Not only did they fail to note the peace and presence of Jesus; they also failed to note the power of Jesus. "Then He arose and rebuked the wind, and said to the sea, 'Peace, be still!' And the wind ceased and there was a great calm" (Mark 4:39). In the Greek language in which the New Testament was originally written, the command of Jesus to the wind is much stronger than can be reflected in the English translation. The statement would be closer if it were translated that Jesus said to the wind, "Will you shut up!" But that isn't the really amazing part—the amazing part is that the wind shut up.

The disciples really should not have been surprised that the wind obeyed Jesus. After all, they had heard the "clank" of the blind beggars' cups hitting the rocks by the side of the road; they had seen the crutches of the cripples thrown in the air; they had seen the dead walking and the lepers cleansed. Should it have been a surprise that Jesus had the power to speak to the wind? Of course not—but it was.

One of the spiritual exercises I have found helpful is the keeping of a spiritual diary. In the diary, I record the times when God has been faithful. When I read the diary, I can find those places where I was scared to death . . . and where God was faithful. I am careful to record those experiences so that the next time I am frightened, I can go back and read the past and say, "If God didn't fail then, He won't fail now." (Or, as my friend, Ken Nanfelt, said to me once, "Steve, if God is going to fail someone, it won't be you. If He fails someone, He will start with Billy Graham or the Pope. You are just a peon.")

The power of Christ is so great that there is nothing outside His control. He is the King. And, because He is the King, I can know that, if things fall apart, it is okay. I don't have to be afraid (or at least as afraid as I am), because He has written the play, He is the director and He knows what He is doing.

There is a great comedy record featuring Mel Brooks as a very old man whose life is measured in thousands of years. The interviewer asks the old man if he was there when people started talking about God. He replied that he was there; and not only that, God's name was Phil. He said that this guy, by the name of Phil, went out into the fields and said that he was God. A lot of people followed him. Then, one day, a lightning bolt came down and killed Phil. Brooks went on to say that the man who was standing next to Phil said, "There's somebody bigger than Phil!" Well, there is somebody bigger than Phil. Christians who are facing fear need to remember that.

How to Handle Fear

Now, the question before the house is this: If we are aware of the peace, the presence and the power of Christ in our lives, what are the implications of that knowledge? In other words: When you are still afraid after realizing the peace, the presence and the power of Christ, what do you do with your fear? I don't have a system, but I do have some helpful suggestions.

Define Your Fear

First, it is important for Christians to define their fear. There is nothing worse than being afraid and not knowing why. What is it that makes you afraid?

- Are you afraid people won't accept you?
- Are you afraid of pain?
- Are you afraid of poverty?
- Are you afraid of death?

Definition is a prerequisite to dealing with fear.

One of the problems with many of us is that we have become so accustomed to our life of fear that we don't know what it is we fear. A man told me once, "Steve, I'm afraid not to be afraid." If you can't make a list of what frightens you, you ought not to be afraid.

I have a lawyer friend who lived a life of fear. Jack (not his real name) was a former alcoholic who found out, when he quit drinking, why he was drinking in the first place. It was his fear. He would call me and list everything that made him want to go back to the bottle. He would say, "Pastor, what if I can't make enough money to feed my family? What if I fail in court? What if I get sick?"

Finally, after listening to my friend's fears on numerous occasions, I said to him, "Jack, let's try an experiment: I want you to write down the ten things that worry you the most. Bring that list of fears to me, and I am going to put that list away in my desk. Six months from now we are going to have lunch together, and we are going to open the envelope and see how many of those fears were realized."

Six months later, my friend called and reminded me about the lunch. To be honest with you, I was worried about that lunch. What if all his fears had become reality? What if my experiment had failed? Nevertheless, we met for lunch and I gave him the envelope, which he opened. Do you know what? Not a single one of the things he had feared had happened!

In the process of defining your fear, it is important that you define the "bottom line" results if the fear becomes a reality. Jesus said,

> For which of you, intending to build a tower, does not sit down first and count the cost, whether he has enough to finish it—lest, after he has laid the foundation, and is not able to finish it, all who see it begin to mock him . . . Or what king, going to make war against another king, does not sit down first and consider whether he is able with ten thousand to meet him who comes against him with twenty thousand? Or else, while the other is still a great way off, he sends a delegation and asks conditions of peace. (Luke 14:28–29, 31–32)

Most of the time, when we define our fear and the costs of the fear's becoming a reality, two things happen. First, we find that, in defining the fear, it is not as great as we first supposed. And second, when we count the cost, we find that, while we would not like to pay the cost, if worse came to worse, we could handle it.

Confess Your Fear

After you define your fear, confess it. Confession is good for the soul . . . and it is good for boldness and freedom too. Honestly bring your fear before God. Tell Him that you are frightened and that you aren't sure you can act because of your fear.

Something I have discovered about boldness is that the Christian's lack of it is always on the "inside" and never perceived on the "outside." In other words, nobody but you, and those you choose to tell, knows you are afraid. Make sure that one of the people you tell is God. The psalmist discovered a great truth: "I sought the LORD, and He heard me, and delivered me from all my fears" (Psalm 34:4).

Fear God Enough

Not only should you define and confess your fear. Third, make sure you fear God enough. "Wait!" you say. "We aren't supposed to fear God; we are supposed to love Him." Yes, we are supposed to love God. But, if you don't find yourself fearing Him, you are probably worshiping an idol. If you have not stood before God and been afraid, you have not stood before God.

The psalmist said, "The fear of the Lord is the beginning of wisdom" (Psalm 111:10). The fear of the Lord is also the beginning of boldness and freedom. John Witherspoon said, "It is only the fear of God that can deliver us from the fear of man."

I am not naturally confrontational. In other words, I would rather switch than fight. I don't like disagreements in the church or anyplace else. Time after time, I have faced tense and frightening situations in the church where I have had to struggle with my need to be loved and my fear of rejection. I have, in the past, occasionally, had to struggle with the issue of whether to say something in the pulpit that needed to be said even if it made people mad.

Given my personality, a betting man would wager that I would not be confrontational. But, let me tell you something interesting. If you were to talk to those who know me, they would tell you that I *am* confrontational—sometimes to the point of being obnoxious. Over and over again, I hear from people, "Don't get Steve angry. It's dangerous."

How have I been able to deal with my need to be loved? I have a need to be loved by the Father more than I have a need to be loved by people. How have I been able to deal with my fear of confrontation? I am more afraid of God than I am of anybody else. I have done it my way and I have done it God's way. God's way is better. I would much rather have people angry at me than to have God angry at me.

Do What You Fear

Finally, go do whatever you fear. There is an old English proverb that says, "Fear knocked at the door, faith answered; and no one was there."

I have a pastor friend who, like me, has difficulty in confronting. He asked if I would help him. Over the course of our many conversations, he told me about a man in his church who had caused serious problems in the fellowship. He had not only intimidated the people in the church (and that was bad enough), but he had also intimidated the pastor (and that can destroy the church). The problem was that he gave a significant amount of money to the church and many of his relatives were in positions of leadership in the church. My pastor friend said, "Steve, I don't know what I can do about him. It would divide the church if I confronted him."

I said, "Let me give you a speech that you should recite to him. Invite this man to your study and say, 'I have had it up to my ears with you. Before this meeting is over, one of us is going to resign.' Then, tell him all the things he has been doing to hurt the church. Tell him, 'This is not your church or my church; this is God's church . . . and He will not allow you to act in this manner anymore.' Then, tell him that you are God's agent to make sure that he doesn't."

My pastor friend turned pale just thinking about it. But the problem was so big that he was willing to do anything. Two days later, my friend called and said, "Steve, you won't believe what has happened. The church member who has been giving the church all the trouble asked if I would forgive him. He said that he knew he had a problem and asked for my help. Not only that, he said that, if I would give him another chance, he would be different. Not only that, his two brothers came in and thanked me for what I did and said that I was the first pastor in twenty years who had had the courage to do what needed doing."

Jesus said that Satan is the father of lies. His "whoppers" are often about what will happen if we stand. Most of the time, we don't find out how big the lie is because we are not willing to call his bluff. But, when you do, the joy of seeing God work in "cleaning up the mess" is one of the great gifts the Father gives to His own.

The point of all the above is this: It's okay to be afraid. It's just not okay to quit.

In practical terms, though, doing what you fear takes great risk. Let me say a few things about that now.

A very wise and bold man once said:

> I do not choose to be a common man. It is my right to be uncom-mon—if I can. I seek opportunity—not security. I do not wish to be a kept citizen, humbled and dulled by having the state look after me. I want to take the calculated risk; to dream and to build; to fail and to succeed. I refuse to barter incentive for a dole. I prefer the challenges of life to the guaranteed existence; the thrill of fulfill-ment to the stale calm of utopia. I will not trade freedom for benefi-cence nor my dignity for a handout. I will never cower before any master nor bend to any threat. It is my heritage to stand erect, proud and unafraid; to think and act for myself; enjoy the benefits of my creations; and to face the world boldly and say, "This I have done." All this is what it means to be free.[23]

That statement refers, of course, to the great power and free-dom to be found in democratic capitalism. It is the kind of quota-tion that causes most of us to feel better about a system of gov-ernment where we can hold our heads up and speak our minds. It is the kind of system where one can enjoy the benefits of suc-cess and accept the responsibilities of failure. It is a call to free-dom, responsibility and integrity.

But the fact is, when you get right down to it, most people are not as interested in freedom as they are in security. Given the clear option between freedom (with its attendant responsibility and problems) and dictatorship (with its attendant structure and limits), most people will pick dictatorship every time. Why? Because we want to be secure and safe, not free and responsible.

The point is this: Freedom sounds good until you get right down to what it costs; and, when that happens, most people will opt for something less than freedom.

Do We Really Want to Be Bold?

In order to conquer your fear and to be willing to risk, you must first ask yourself the question: *Do I really want to be bold?* It is just as true in religion as it is in politics. Most of us would rather have someone else tell us what God says than to listen to God speaking; most of us would rather read a commentary than the Bible; most of us would rather be in submission to a religious authority figure than to take responsibility ourselves; most of us would rather listen to a sermon than preach one. Someone has said that many Christians are running around with an umbilical cord looking for a place to plug it in.

And so, it seems to me, it is important before we go any further in our pursuit of Christian boldness that we decide whether we *want* Christian boldness. I heard about a speaker who was addressing a conference of Christian athletes who said, "You think I have come here to make you feel better. That isn't true. I have come here to bind up the wounds from the last battle before I send you out to the next one."

Someone tells the story of a college football team that was losing an important game by a wide margin. The coach stood on the sidelines yelling to his team, "Give the ball to Jack! Give the ball to Jack!" But Jack never got the ball, and the team continued to lose. The coach yelled again, "Give the ball to Jack!"

One of the players finally yelled back to the coach, "Jack says he doesn't want the ball!"

You may simply not want the ball. Better to decide that now than later, because there is no one more miserable than the person who is reaching for someone else's goal.

I spend a portion of my time teaching seminary students, and one of the pastoral traits that I urge my students to develop is a "mean streak." One of the problems in many American churches is that pastors have become "free bait" for neurotic (and they are a small minority) church members. If the members don't like the way a pastor parts his hair or ties his tie, they feel free to tell him. If they don't like his wife's dress, they tell him. If they don't like the way he smiles, they tell him. I could write a book on the comments people make to a pastor, comments they would never think of making to anybody else. (This is one of the reasons I'm glad I'm no longer a pastor!)

Not too long ago, I was talking to a pastor who was in some serious trouble with his congregation. He was being criticized and made fun of in a shameful way. As we talked, it became apparent to me that it was necessary for this young man to develop a "mean streak" or he wasn't going to survive. He told me that he felt he had been called to "love" his people and to understand them even when they were cruel and abusive. I said to him that, while I felt he should be loving and kind, it was very important that he be honest and strong too. I suggested that he bring the people who had been making the comments before the ruling body of the church and call them either to refrain from such comments in the future or to justify their disturbance of the peace and unity of the church.

That young pastor made a very interesting comment to me. He said, "Steve, I know that is what I should do, but I'm just not made that way. I feel my ministry is to pour oil on troubled waters, not put a match to it." Needless to say, that young man is no longer in the ministry. He didn't have enough oil for all the troubled waters. He is now selling insurance.

The Price of Boldness

When the Christian gets serious about Christian boldness and freedom, there is a price to pay.

If you decide to go the way of boldness, what is it going to cost you? We have already talked about the price tag of fear; let's now talk about the price tag of risk.

Risk Sometimes Ends in Failure

First, Christian boldness presupposes that you will sometimes fail because you are required to risk. The easiest way I know to avoid failure is never to risk. In my pagan days, I played a lot of poker. As a matter of fact, you can learn a lot about life and people from playing poker. Kenny Rogers wasn't the only one to discover that. When you play poker and you are never willing to risk, you must face the prospect that you will never win. Most people who play poker and never risk may be down a little one week and up a little the next week, but they will never have the satisfaction of taking a large "pot." Life is like that. If you never risk saying something inappropriate, if you never risk a relationship by telling the truth, if you never risk the acceptance of your friends by being faithful to Christ, then you will be safe; but you will never know the excitement and the great rewards of risk.

There is a popular minister in this country who is often the butt of jokes and criticism. He continues to succeed; and, the more he succeeds, the more he is criticized. A friend of mine recently wrote him a note after a very critical article had appeared in a prominent magazine. My friend wrote, "If you are tired of the criticism, there is a very easy way to bring it to a stop. Simply fail."

Well, that is not entirely accurate. As a matter of fact, if he should have significant failure, the criticism would not stop. However, if he had never tried to succeed, he would never have been criticized.

One of the important points I try to make with seminary students is that, if they are in doubt about saying something in the pulpit, they ought to say it. When I say that, there are often questions from the students. They wonder if that isn't a bit radical; they wonder if maybe that kind of thing could lead to saying something improper in the pulpit; they think a lot of people will get upset. I always say, "Yes, all of that is true. However, if you risk, the people who sit under your ministry will never sleep and you will find that, much of the time, it was in the area of risk that you communicated truth in a way the people could hear and understand."

Martin Luther said that if we sin we ought to "sin boldly." What did he mean by that? He meant that there is nothing worse than a Christian who cowers over in a corner, whining about the perils of the pagan world. For God's sake, I think Luther would say, "Quit whining and do something—even if it is done badly."

I live in a large city and, when you live in a city, you begin to think a lot about safety. You can put bars on your windows, spotlights in your yard and bolts on your doors. You can buy a big dog, a big gun and a big fence. You can set up a security system that no one can break and "Keep Out, Bad Dog" signs that no one but a fool would ignore. You can refuse to go for a walk or risk speaking to a stranger. You can have police patrolling the neighborhood and neighbors you are afraid to know. You can do all of that; but, the problem is that, once you have done it all, you are no different from the man who is in a solitary confinement cell. He is usually safe too, but his freedom is gone.

One of the things I have noticed about a lot of Christians is that they are afraid to risk checking out their faith against the arguments of unbelievers. They operate on the general principle that, while their faith may not be much, it is all they've got. If they challenge a pagan, the pagan may rob them of the little they have . . . so they just remain quiet.

At the church I once served, we sometimes had what we called "Skeptics' Forum." We invited atheists and agnostics to come and meet with the pastor (me) to find some honest answers to their honest questions. We made the promise that no one would beat them over the head with a Bible or pray over them (at least in their presence). I was the only Christian allowed in the room, and the meeting was usually held in my study. The skeptics set the format by listing the subjects they wanted to discuss and each evening, I would talk for about ten minutes on the particular subject. Then, for the next two hours, the skeptics were given a chance to go after me.

The first Skeptics' Forum was extremely frightening for me. I thought these unbelievers had a deep, thoughtful commitment to their unbelief. As a matter of fact, just the opposite was true. Most skeptics' intellectual acumen is about as shallow as a child's wading pool. The hardest thing about Skeptics' Forum was to refrain from saying, "That is the dumbest thing I have ever heard. I can't believe you would say something as stupid as that!" Of course, I never said anything like that, but I was reminded of Billy Sunday's comment that "a sinner can repent, but stupid is forever."

From the forum, I learned it was only in risking that I discovered the truth of my faith. If I had never risked, I probably would have held on to the little faith that I professed, but I would have always wondered if it were true. Its truth was discovered in risk.

If you want to exercise free, bold Christianity, you have to be prepared to face the possibility of failure, because you have to risk. Too many Christians refuse to risk politically, socially or spiritually. They have traded a prison called security for the excitement of standing on the "firing line."

Some People Won't Like You

Second, if you decide to be a bold Christian, you have to face the reality that not everyone is going to like you. Most of us have a great need to be loved; and, because of that need, many of us sell our souls. We commit some of our worst and most sinful acts simply because we want to be loved.

Amma Sarah, one of the desert Christians of the fourth and fifth centuries, said, "If I prayed God that all men should approve of my conduct, I should find myself a penitent at the door of each one, but I shall rather pray that my heart may be pure towards all."[24]

One of the hardest lessons I ever learned was that I can't please everyone. I want to; I want to be what everyone wants me to be; I want everyone to love me. The problem is that it simply can't be done. It is the problem with a lot of Christians. We believe spurious doctrines, refuse to ask questions, are afraid to confront, stifle protests, keep quiet when we ought to speak, allow ourselves to be manipulated—all because we are afraid that people won't love us if we don't please them.

There is a crisis in this country among pastors who have a need to be liked. I can understand that because it was one of my problems too. Have you ever noticed the Christian liturgy that takes place, not during the worship service, but after it? The pastor goes to the front door of the church and everyone files past him. As they pass him, the liturgy requires that they say, "Pastor, that was a wonderful sermon." The liturgy then requires that the pastor respond by saying, "Thank you for saying that. I'm pleased that God used it."

Now, I suspect this practice is fine except when the pastor has preached a "bomb." He knows it and the congregation knows it too. During the sermon, people were checking their watches . . . and then they were shaking them to make sure they weren't broken! Everybody was bored and the sermon died before it got to the first pew. Never mind—the Christian liturgy is chiseled in concrete; the pastor still has to go to the front door and the people still have to file past him with the same comment and the same response.

If you are not a pastor, you won't understand how terrible those times are. The problem comes, however, when a pastor wants, more than anything in the world, to avoid those kinds of days. He begins to write his sermons to please his congregation. He knows there is truth that needs to be said, but he doesn't say it because it might offend someone. The pastor knows he needs to be strong; but, if he is too strong, people might be upset, so he passes out pious pablum that doesn't offend anyone.

Because a pastor's self-identity is so caught up in what he does in the pulpit, it isn't a long distance between being kind, sweet and insipid in the pulpit and being kind, sweet and insipid in every area of his life.

I once read a book with a great title: *Bible in Pocket, Gun in Hand.* It was about the frontier preachers in America and their determination to preach the gospel whether or not anybody wanted to listen. They would have been very uncomfortable in many contemporary churches. In fact, most of our churches would have been uncomfortable with them. They simply would not have been able to play the game.

But, lest you think I am just talking about a clergy problem, let me say that the average Christian wants to be loved too. That desire causes more Christians to keep quiet at inappropriate times than anything I know.

During the "Jesus Movement" of the sixties and early seventies, I was the pastor of a Presbyterian church near Boston. We were the big Presbyterian church up on the hill; and, if nothing else, we were certainly proper. And then Jesus began sending some rather smelly, unkempt, vocal young Christians into our fellowship. I must say that the dear people in that church, its pastor included, did quite well in accepting those kids. But, to be perfectly honest with you, it wasn't easy.

I remember one time when they decided to have a "Jesus March" around the church before the Sunday morning worship service. They made "Jesus" signs, printed up "Jesus" T-shirts and carried "Jesus" banners. They got all the kids in the Sunday school to march with them. Now that was rather difficult for Presbyterians to absorb by itself; but, when they started the "Jesus" yell, it almost brought the whole thing to an end. (It went, "Give me a 'J,' give me an 'E,' give me an 'S,'" and so on.) You could hear the yell all over the neighborhood. I thought, *What will people think? What will the elderly people coming to church during the march think? What do I think?*

Occasionally, during the Sunday evening service, I would ask a few of those young people to stand before the congregation and tell what Christ had done for them. You should have heard some of those little speeches. They talked about their rebellion, their drugs, their guilt and how Jesus had changed everything. The problem was that their language was rather graphic. To be perfectly honest with you, graphic language has no place in a Presbyterian church, but I let them continue because what they were saying was so real. There were times when I hid in the chair behind the big column to the right of the pulpit and prayed nervously, "Lord, help him/her to say it in a way that is a little softer." But they never did.

During those days, and they were exciting, I discovered what made those "Jesus people" so winsome. They cared more for what Jesus thought than for what anybody else thought. That was a good lesson for me and for the congregation.

If you are going to be bold and free, you have to face the fact that a lot of people won't understand. If you are going to be different, you must realize before you decide to be different that most people want you to be like them; and, if you aren't, they won't like it. Count that cost before you decide to be different.

You Might Lose Your Peace

And then there is another cost that must be paid if you decide to become a bold Christian: It will sometimes rob you of your peace. "Wait," you say, "I thought that Jesus gave peace in the midst of turmoil. The least I could expect is personal peace in the conflict." Yes, that is true, but you need to know the kind of peace about which Jesus spoke.

First, let me give you a principle: The peace this side of conflict is not worth a hill of beans. In fact, it is not the kind of peace about which Jesus spoke. The peace this side of conflict is not biblical peace at all; it is simply apathetic contentment. If you want to be contented like a cow, drink lots of milk and keep your mouth shut. Only dead people and cows know that kind of peace.

In contrast, whereas the peace on this side of conflict is not worth a bag of chicken feed, the peace on the other side of conflict is worth anything it costs you.

Have you ever heard those Christians who say they know God's will because they "feel peace" about it? I don't want to say that isn't the way to know God's will, but let me tell you about my experience. I have never felt peace about anything that was God's will. In fact, the place of my greatest turmoil and conflict has often come when I was in God's will.

I want you to go with me to the garden of Gethsemane, where a Man by the name of Jesus was about to die. He knew He was going to die and He knew that the death He faced was going to be horrible.

When a man is frightened, he wants someone with him. Jesus was God; but He was also a man and He asked His disciples to stay with Him as He prayed. Matthew told the story:

> Then Jesus came with them to a place called Gethsemane, and said to the disciples, "Sit here while I go and pray over there." And He took with Him Peter and the two sons of Zebedee, and He began to be sorrowful and deeply distressed. Then He said to them, "My soul is exceedingly sorrowful, even to death. Stay here and watch with Me." He went a little farther and fell on His face, and prayed, saying "O My Father, if it is possible, let this cup pass from Me; nevertheless, not as I will, but as You will." (Matthew 26:36–39)

The physician Luke with his practiced medical eye said, "And being in agony, He prayed more earnestly. And His sweat became like great drops of blood falling down to the ground" (Luke 22:44).

Now, if you think Jesus felt peace in that garden as He prepared to face the cross, I have some land to sell you in the middle of a swamp in Florida. He was not peaceful, and if Jesus was not peaceful when He was in the center of the will of God, why in the world do we think we should feel peaceful when we are in the center of the will of God?

But, on the other side of the conflict, we see a peace that is nothing less than supernatural. When Jesus was dying, He prayed for those who killed Him to be forgiven and His final words were, "Father, into Your hands I commend My spirit" (Luke 23:46).

If you decide to be different, to stand, to risk, the resultant "feeling" might well be, "I wish I had kept my mouth shut. How could I have been so stupid?" But, as time passes, there will be a peace that you have never known, a peace that says, "I didn't like what I did. It made me feel out of sorts and anxious. But I did what God said." At night, in those few minutes just before sleep, you will be able to "rest easy" and "sleep clean" with the peace of one who has been faithful.

As you decide to use your fear and to risk becoming a free and bold Christian, I'm not going to promise you success, acceptance and peace. You have to pay a price for anything of value. However, I do promise that ultimate success will be yours, that the Father will accept you even if no one else does and that, when it comes your time to die, you will be able to say, "Father, I did what you told me to do."

Someone tells the story of the missionary who came back to America after an extended mission tour. He was Christ's faithful servant and it was good to get home. It happened that he was on the same ship that was bringing Theodore Roosevelt back to New York from an overseas trip. There was a great crowd at the dock; and, at first, the missionary thought they had come to welcome him. But soon it became apparent that they had gathered for Roosevelt.

As Roosevelt walked off the ship onto the dock, the band started playing and people started shouting. The crowd lifted Roosevelt on their shoulders and marched off down the street. The missionary then made his way to the dock. He was alone. He had tears in his eyes and he prayed, "Father, I have been serving you all these years. I've been faithful. I have proclaimed your message. But, when this man comes home, he has a band and a crowd. When

I come home, there is no one to meet me, no one to shout, no one to make me feel welcome."

It was then that the missionary heard the voice. It was a voice he knew intimately. It was the voice of the God he served. He heard the words he would remember until the day he died: "Son, you aren't Home yet."

7

A Program

Assertiveness Training for Christians

Now we are going to get down and talk about, in a very practical way, how to be a bold, free Christian. We have already covered the definition of boldness and the problems of boldness. But that is not enough. Now I want to share the how-to: assertiveness training for Christians.

Before we do that, though, let me say something about those relationships which are worth the effort of honesty and confrontation. The fact is, boldness is very difficult. Confrontation is hard.

Jesus said in John 15:15, "No longer do I call you servants, for a servant does not know what his master is doing; but I have called you friends, for all things that I heard from My Father I have made known to you."

If you want to be bold, it is important, first, to determine the people to whom to be bold. The principle of relationships is this: *Honesty and confrontation increase in direct proportion to the closeness of relationship.*

There are four levels of relationships: Colleague relationships, casual relationships, familiar relationships and intimate relationships. Most relationships take great emotional effort—to confront, to be bold and to be honest. One exception, though. When there is boldness—and I expect there will be boldness in all of your relationships—it won't cost you anything to be bold with a casual acquaintance.

One more thing before we turn to the 10 Commandments of Boldness: We must take a moment to define the difference between being in pain, a pain, a pain in the neck and a pain reliever.

To be in pain, as we examine assertiveness, is to be suffering from the wimp syndrome. There is great pain in never saying what you feel, in always submitting to others and in failing to say "no" when you should. This chapter is designed to help you deal with that kind of pain.

Some people are, by their very nature, just pains. As W. C. Fields said, "I'm not prejudiced. I hate everybody." There are some people who don't need assertiveness training, they need gentleness training. This training in assertiveness should not be used as an excuse for a mean-spirited personality.

When I wrote my original book on boldness, *No More Mr. Nice Guy*, my daughter, Robin, read the manuscript. Joking, I said to her (she doesn't need assertiveness training!), "Honey, you don't need to read that book. You need to read a book on being a nice person."

Later, Robin told a friend what I had said. The friend responded, "And who's going to write it? Certainly *not* your father!"

Then, there are those who are a pain in the neck. One of the difficulties with assertiveness training is that, like judo, you want to go out and use it as quickly as possible. You start looking for people to get.

One time, a former Mormon wanted to join a church where I was the pastor. She had been a real leader in Mormonism, head of women's groups as well as a teacher. I asked this woman why she wanted to become a Presbyterian, to which she immediately replied, "I can't stand my husband! The Mormons teach that I will be married to him for all of eternity. I could stand it, I suppose, until I died, but I just can't stand it for all of eternity!"

I told the woman that that probably wasn't a good reason to become a Presbyterian and asked her to hang around awhile before joining.

What was the woman's problem? She tried to fix a problem immediately. When you first hear about assertiveness and become convinced that it is biblically correct, you have to be careful in the same way a new Christian has to be careful. You don't go out and beat everyone you know over the head.

Finally, you can be a pain reliever. *The difference between a wimp, a monster and a bold Christian is that a wimp underreacts, a monster overreacts and a bold Christian acts clearly and definitely, with power and love.*

A bold Christian is a Christian who seeks to control himself or herself . . . not others. It is living a life of honesty and directness before pagans as well as before your brothers and sisters in Christ. In that sense, while boldness may hurt those who would control you, in the long run it creates an atmosphere of truth and understanding. Because that is so, the bold Christian is a pain reliever.

Now, as an introduction to this program of boldness, let me give you a basic principle of behavioral psychology. In some cases, I have some problems with behavioral psychology, but this principle is accurate and helpful when one is dealing with assertiveness. The principle is this: *What you do influences who you are and how you feel about yourself. By changing what you do, you change who you are.*

Because I believe that principle is true, what follows is some help in changing behavior. If you change your behavior, you will find that the role you play will become the reality. You will act like a bold Christian and will, thus, become a bold Christian.

Now, let's turn to assertiveness training—the 10 Commandments of the bold Christian.

Thou Shalt Communicate Clearly

First, thou shalt communicate clearly. Once again, in Matthew 5:37, Jesus said:

But let your "Yes" be "Yes," and your "No," "No." For whatever is more than these is from the evil one.

Communication is the key to all Christian boldness. From the Rule of St. Benedict, 6th century, A.D.:

> If any pilgrim monk come from distant parts, with wish as a guest to dwell in the monastery, and will be content with the customs which he finds in the place, and do not perchance by his lavishness disturb the monastery, but is simply content with what he finds, he shall be received, for as long a time as he desires. If, indeed, he find fault with anything, or expose it, reasonably, and with the humility of charity, the abbot shall discuss it prudently, lest perchance God has sent him for this very thing. But if he has been found gossipy and contumacious in the time of his sojourn as guest, not only ought he not to be joined to the body of the monastery, but also it shall be said to him, honestly, that he must depart. If he does not go, let two stout monks, in the name of God, explain the matter to him.

Now, I, of course, don't necessarily advocate that kind of communication! Christians do, though, need to be very careful to communicate what they want to say in a way that can be clearly understood by the person to whom they communicate.

In marriage counseling, I often conduct a communication experiment between the husband and wife with me serving as the referee. There is one rule: "Talk to each other, in turn, but the one who listens cannot respond until he or she tells the other what has just been communicated and the spouse agrees."

You wouldn't believe what happens. I usually let the wife go first and, the entire time, the husband keeps trying to interrupt. She blasts him and then he starts to blast her right back.

I calmly remind the husband, "Wait just a moment. You have to tell her what she just said and then she has to agree."

The husband will say, "I *know* what she said."

"Then," I will say, "tell her what she just said."

The husband will tell his wife what she supposedly said, to which she responds, "That isn't what I was saying at all!"

I say, "Then tell him again."

Usually the experiment ends up being quite humorous! The point of the lack of communication between the couple is made very clearly.

I teach communication at Reformed Seminary and it absolutely amazes me to find out how little of what is communicated is actually understood.

Let me give you some very simple and important rules:

- Short and succinct messages are always best—Just say what you think and don't try to explain. The fact is, explanation often confuses communication.
- Catch words ("in" jargon) don't communicate well.
- Say what you mean and mean what you say—It is a good practice to check your communication by asking the other person, "Sometimes, I don't communicate well. Will you tell me what you think I just said?"
- Negative communications are best when they are short and without sugar.
- Writing it down is often a way of clearly saying what you want to say.
- And finally: When you have communicated clearly, don't allow another person's poor listening skills to be a way he or she manipulates you.

Thou Shalt Repudiate Absolutely

The second commandment: Thou shalt repudiate absolutely.

And when they had brought them, they set them before the council. And the high priest asked them, saying, "Did we not strictly command you not to teach in this name? And look, you have filled Jerusalem with your doctrine, and intend to bring this Man's blood on us!" But Peter and the other apostles answered and said: "We ought to obey God rather than men." (Acts 5:27–29)

In almost everything important in your life, it is necessary to "draw a line in the sand." Too many Christians have not made the decision on where to draw that line.

If you are not sure when you became a Christian, sometimes it is good to hammer it down. Pick a date, like today, and say "I became a Christian on this date, if not before." One of the good things about having an invitation during a worship service is the fact that one hammers down the commitment by coming forward. It is important to draw the line in the sand.

One of the things I teach seminary students is to recognize that they *will* compromise. Whenever I say that, the students look at me as if I've lost my mind. The problem is that they are young and haven't yet compromised on a lot of things. However, the nature of life is that there are a lot of compromises. Sometimes I can't tell people the whole truth because it would simply devastate them.

At any rate, I tell the students to decide those places in which they will not compromise, to write it down and to consult the list often.

Corrie ten Boom's sister was faced with a compromise when the Nazis came to see if there were any Jews in her home. She could have lied, saving the Jews' lives, or she could have told the truth, condemning the Jews to the concentration camp.

It is a similar situation with the institution of the church. Sometimes, you have to be nice when the bills need to be paid, but there should be a place where one draws the line.

There was a man in a church I once served who gave $5,000 to the building program. The problem was that he felt that his $5,000 gave him permission to direct the entire building program. (As a matter of fact, a whole lot of people gave more and gave more sacrificially than he did!) Every Sunday, the man came into my study, complaining about something going on in the building program.

One Sunday, Jack (and that's not his real name) came in just as the elders were meeting for prayer and said something stupid about the building program. I said to him, "Jack, that's it! That is all your $5,000 will buy you. If you want to give more money to this building program, I will listen to more of your nonsense, but you have just run out of your original gift."

The elders were shocked. He left the church and the church was better off. In other words, I drew the line.

In counseling about sexual matters, I often tell young people to decide what they're going to do about sex before they're faced with the opportunity. If they don't decide beforehand, I tell them, passion will take over and they will do what comes naturally. If the decision about where to end the date (in the bedroom or the living room) is not made before the end of the date, the date will always end in the bedroom.

And so, if you are going to become a bold and free Christian, the place to start is to make a list of "nevers" for your life. Put that list in the front of your Bible and check it often.

Everyone's list will be different because we are all at different places and we all have different personalities, but the rule is the same: If you don't draw a line in the sand, your enemy will cross it every time.

Let me make a few suggestions for your list of "nevers":

1. Never grovel.
2. Never apologize when you are right.
3. Never say "no" more than twice.
4. Never lie.
5. Never pretend to be someone's mother.
6. Never take responsibility for what is not your responsibility.

Once you have drawn the line in the sand, only then to violate your own rules, ask for forgiveness and draw the line again . . . until it becomes absolute.

Thou Shalt Report Honestly

The third commandment is this: Thou shalt report honestly.

For we are God's fellow workers . . . (1 Corinthians 3:9)

I am glad about the coming of Stephanas, Fortunatus, and Achaicus, for what was lacking on your part they supplied. (1 Corinthians 16:17)

Let me give you a biblical truth: *No Christian is ever bold by himself or herself.* Accountability in all matters in general, and in boldness in particular, is an absolute necessity for escaping from the wimp syndrome.

A number of years ago, I was invited to be the after dinner speaker at the annual banquet for the South Shore Men's Club in Boston. They had heard about my reputation for telling jokes and for talking about love, peace and joy. What they didn't know is that, subsequent to my achieving that reputation, I had found Jesus Christ. Now I had more than jokes to give.

When the president called, I decided to be honest with him. I explained that I had found Christ and that I now talked about Christ whenever I spoke.

"I realize," I said to the president, "that you may not have signed on for this and, because I don't have any ego invested, why don't you go back to your board and check it out. If you would rather have someone else, I will understand perfectly."

The next day, the president called and said, "Reverend Brown, we voted for you to come and you can say whatever you want. The vote was five to four."

When I got there, it was a big auditorium with the booze flowing freely. People were having a very good time. Not only that, the man sitting on my right and the man sitting on my left were playing a game peculiar to laymen called "Shock the Reverend," telling dirty jokes, over my head, to one another. (I thought that I would play the game of "Shock the Laymen," and say to them, "Look, I know all those jokes better than you do, and certainly can tell them better. Why don't you let me tell them?" Of course, I didn't say that!)

At any rate, as I listened to the jokes and saw the evening deteriorate, I said to myself, *Myself, I think what you were going to say is a little strong. Maybe back off a bit. Tell a few jokes and make everyone feel good.*

But, just at that moment and just before I was to go to the speaker's platform, an elder in the church I then served, walked up the long auditorium. He came up behind me, put his hand strongly on my shoulder and whispered in my ear, "Pastor, don't you back off one bit. I'm praying for you."

The power of accountability. It may be your wife or husband. It may be a close friend who is dealing with the same problem you are. Whoever it is, you need to have someone with whom you can be accountable.

One time, I had a Christian education director in a church I served who was being attacked at every board of Christian education meeting. He just took it and, as a result, the situation only got worse.

Finally, I told the director, "John, I would be glad to tell them to hang it on their ear for you, but that wouldn't help you any and you would feel terrible. I don't mind fighting your battles for you; but, in this case, I think it is important that you fight it yourself. Not only that, I'm going to hold you accountable. If you allow them to go after you again without saying anything, you are going to be looking for another job tomorrow. I'm going to check in the morning."

The next morning, he looked like the world had been lifted off his shoulders. The Christian education director said to me, "Steve, I told them that I wasn't going to listen to their criticism anymore. In fact, I told them that I wasn't going to resign; so, if they wanted any peace, they should leave the board. Nobody left and we had a wonderful meeting!"

Find a kindred spirit and be accountable.

Thou Shalt Practice Faithfully

The fourth commandment of Christian boldness is this: Thou shalt practice faithfully. Take a look at Paul's words in Galatians:

I marvel that you are turning away so soon from Him who called you in the grace of Christ, to a different gospel. (1:6)

But it is good to be zealous in a good thing always, and not only when I am present with you. (4:18)

Be faithful in whatever situation you find yourself.

My friend, Fred Smith, says that practice doesn't make perfect; only correct practice makes perfect. Incorrect practice only ingrains the error.

If you have been suffering from the wimp syndrome and now have become a bold Christian, know that you will be uncomfortable for a while. The more you stand, though, the easier it will become. That is a fact and a promise. Remember it when you start the process.

Let me give you some direction. First, pray that the Lord will put you in situations where you can be bold and ask Him to let you know about the situation before it is too late. Second, plan how you will react to those situations. And then, third, practice.

Here are some practice situations:

- Practice saying "no" without giving an explanation or trying to justify your "no."
- Watch lines in supermarkets. When someone steps in front of you, practice saying, "Excuse me, but I was here before you."
- Think of someone who irritates you and practice telling him or her so.
- Write at least one letter each year to your local newspaper, disagreeing with their editorial policy.
- Tell your pastor, lovingly, at least once a year, about something with which you disagreed in his sermon.
- Don't defend yourself to your children.
- Plan to take a stand on some issue and don't give in, for peace's sake.

That is a good start. You will probably feel very nervous the first time you practice, but stay with it. The more you stand, the easier it will become.

I have a very shy friend who wanted, more than anything else in the world, to share his faith. He had never done it before and it became a difficult area of failure in his life. My friend planned what he was going to say and how he was going to say it, only to give up at the last moment. It was as if he walked around with a loaded gun, afraid to pull the trigger.

I'll never forget the night we visited a friend in the hospital. There was another patient in the room who was not a Christian and quite verbal about it.

I had been talking to our friend and getting ready to have a prayer, when I heard, from the direction of the other bed, my reticent friend say, "And you're going to hell unless you do something about it." I turned around and saw my friend sharing his faith.

Now, my friend was too blunt and not very sophisticated about it, but, he had shared his faith. When we walked out into the parking lot that evening, my friend began shouting, "I did it! I did it!"

You can have the same experience of joy if you put into practice a policy of boldness.

Thou Shalt Evaluate Realistically

The fifth commandment: Thou shalt evaluate realistically. We have looked at Luke 14:28–31 in the last chapter, but let's look at it again in this context. Jesus says:

> For which of you, intending to build a tower, does not sit down first and count the cost, whether he has enough to finish it—lest, after he has laid the foundation, and is not able to finish it, all who see it begin to mock him, saying, "This man began to build and was not able to finish." Or what king, going to make war against another king, does not sit down first and consider whether he is able with ten thousand to meet him who comes against him with twenty thousand?

If you have been trapped in the wimp syndrome for a long time, it is terribly important that you set realistic goals and that you not be too hard on yourself when you take your first halting steps in the direction of becoming a bold Christian.

I have a pastor friend who is, by nature, very gentle and loving. He simply wouldn't hurt a fly. A situation in his church became terrible and the health of the whole congregation was at stake. My pastor friend called to ask me what he should do about those who were causing the problem in the church. I told him to tell them where to go. (Well, I was more specific than that!)

The next day, my pastor friend called me and said, "Steve, I took your advice and they are really angry. What should I do now?"

It took us, working together, almost six months to get the mess straightened out.

What's the point? Just this: Be realistic about who is going to get burned by the fires you start. In other words, plan very carefully and never, never use a cannon to kill a fly.

For example, if you are being manipulated by a parent, don't tell them to "hang it on their ear." Say something like, "Mother, I want you to know that the next time you say that kind of thing to me, I will tell you that I love you and then I will walk away."

Make sure, in this type of situation, to evaluate realistically.

Thou Shalt Envision Regularly

Now to the sixth commandment: Thou shalt envision regularly. Paul, after describing to King Agrippa his vision on the road to Damascus where God commissioned him, said this, "Therefore, King Agrippa, I was not disobedient to the heavenly vision" (Acts 26:19).

Paul also taught:

And do not be conformed to this world, but be transformed by the renewing of your mind, that you may prove what is that good and acceptable and perfect will of God. (Romans 12:2)

You need to know that, when I began working on this point, the word I originally used was "imagine." The commandment is this: *Thou shalt imagine regularly.* But, of course, I couldn't use the word "imagine" because of the New Age . . . and, to be honest with you, that ticks me off. I am so tired of the New Age robbing Christians of perfectly biblical and healthy ways of being obedient to God. Visualization is wrong, but visualizing what God would have you to become is perfectly legitimate.

Let me give you a principle: You have an image of yourself. That is an inescapable fact. The only question is not whether or not you will have an image; but, rather, what that image is, good or bad.

I teach the seminary students to visualize themselves preaching with great power and freedom, speaking boldly, teaching God's Word and seeing lives changed. When the students do that, they preach with more power and freedom than they had before. The fact is, if they didn't have that vision, they would have another one.

It is the same thing with becoming bold. Get out a piece of paper and ask yourself, "If I were bold, secure and assertive, what would I be like and what would I do?" Be very specific and write it down. After you write it down, close your eyes and imagine yourself being that way. Then pray, "Father, I know you want me to be bold. If all that I've written down and imagined is from you, give me your grace to become what you have called me to become."

When I was in junior high school and in the marching band, the man who directed the band was also the coach. For some reason, Mr. Smith (not his real name) disliked me. He had served as a drill sergeant in the Marines. Day after day, Mr. Smith yelled at me, "Brown, you don't know your left from your right. I'm going to put a brick on your left shoulder so you can tell!" or "Brown, you are out of line again. You are the worst marcher I have ever seen!"

Over the summer, just before my last year at that school, I grew . . . and grew. The year before, I started out the shortest boy in the band and, then over the summer, I became the tallest boy. All that summer, I dreaded going back to school because I knew what was going to happen in band. I knew I was going to be embarrassed and hurt over and over again . . . and I didn't know what to do about it.

So, I started having this dream of standing up to Mr. Smith. I was going to, with respect, tell him that I wasn't going to put up with his treatment anymore. I thought about it all summer, picturing myself strong.

So, what happened? At the end of the summer, the band met on the field and we started our first march around the field. You are right, that turkey started on me again! With trembling, I simply stopped marching and let the band go on around me.

Before my adversary could yell at me again, I went over to him and said, "Mr. Smith, I'm not going through another year like the last one. You have picked on me and picked on me and I'm not going to take it anymore. If it happens again, I'm going to my parents and then we're going to the principal."

Mr. Smith turned red in the face and yelled, "Brown, get back in that line this minute!" I did. The funny thing was that, after that, he never yelled at me again.

If you were bold, what would you be like? Be that way.

Thou Shalt Persevere Faithfully

The seventh commandment: Thou shalt persevere faithfully. Take a look at Paul's words to the church at Corinth:

I was with you in weakness, in fear, and in much trembling [but, parenthetically, I was with you]. (1 Corinthians 2:3)

Therefore, since we have this ministry, as we have received mercy, we do not lose heart. (2 Corinthians 4:1)

I've said it before and I'll say it again now: *It is okay to be afraid, but it is not okay to quit.* One of the reasons most Christians aren't bold is because they simply don't feel bold. They see other Christians who say what they mean and mean what they say, only to think that those Christians are different. They aren't. They are just like you.

Marshall Ney, Napoleon's right-hand man in battle, was one of the most courageous men who ever lived. Before he would go into battle, Ney would look down at his shaking legs and say, "Shake, will you? If you knew where I was taking you today, you would shake even more."

Boldness and freedom will create all kinds of fear in you. You will be afraid that people won't like you, that you will be rejected and that you will be attacked. You will also be afraid that people's feelings will get hurt. That is all okay, though. Why? Because it is okay to be afraid; it is just not okay to quit.

When my friend, Ron Minor, was the pastor at a church in Cambridge, Massachusetts, he once had an appointment with a Harvard professor. The professor was late for the meeting. While Ron sat and waited in the man's book-lined office, a voice said to him, "Ron, tell the professor that I love him."

"But, Father, he will think I'm crazy!"

Once again, the voice: "Ron, tell the professor that I love him and that my Son died for his sins."

"But Lord, you don't understand. He already thinks that I'm some kind of Bible-thumping Fundamentalist."

"Ron, tell him that I love him."

So, with great fear, Ron, in a simple and childlike way, told this professor about Christ's death on the cross for sin and about God's love for him. That day, there was a new name in the Book of Life.

Remember: *It is okay to be afraid; it is not okay to quit.*

The next time you want to tell someone what you really think, ignore the fear and say it. The next time you want to say "no" without explanation, ignore the fear and say "no." The next time you are reticent about expressing your views, ignore the fear and express those views. The next time people try to manipulate you with guilt and intimidation, ignore the fear and don't let them. One more time: It is okay to be afraid, but it is not okay to quit.

Thou Shalt Forgive Easily

The eighth commandment: Thou shalt forgive easily. What does the Bible teach?

> And be kind to one another, tenderhearted, forgiving one another, as God in Christ forgave you. (Ephesians 4:32)

Valuable relationships are created only out of the stuff of forgiveness. If you want to go deeper, you have to learn to forgive. There is no such thing as a good friendship or an intimate relationship in which perfect people get along.

If you have ever done small group work or have been involved in a small group, then you know that the small group never goes very deep until there is some kind of explosion. Likewise, a church in which everybody is nice is a dead church. A marriage in which there is no fighting is a dead marriage.

One of the problems with most marriages, as well as most other relationships, is the problem of "gunny sacking." Gunny sacking is when you're so angry or upset about something in a relationship that you want to say something, but don't. You put it in a gunny sack and, after a while, the gunny sack gets so heavy that you can't carry it anymore. So, you take the sack off your back and throw it in your friend's face. That will destroy a relationship.

Let me illustrate with a new marriage. The couple have only been married three months when the young wife decides to come home early from work and to make the evening very special. She cooks his favorite meal, sets candles on the table and dresses in her most fetching outfit.

Then the husband, without telling his wife, stops off for a beer with the boys. He shows up two hours late. She says to herself, *I could kill him! He is the most insensitive clod I have ever known. But, we have only been married for a short time. If I yell at him, the neighbors will hear and our witness will be hurt. Besides, I do love him.* So, the wife makes the best out of a bad evening.

Then, suppose, the next morning, the husband has an important, early appointment. The wife tries to wake him up, but he turns over and goes back to sleep. Finally, she takes a cup of cold water and pours it all over him. The husband comes out of bed like a bear, thinking to himself, *That woman, I can't believe she did that to me. I could kill her! But then he thinks, I did have an appointment. If I say what I want to as loudly as I want, the neighbors will hear and it will hurt our witness. And, after all, I do love her.* So, the husband dries himself off and gets dressed.

And then, that night, somebody leaves the cap off the toothpaste tube and, very quickly, there is a third world war over the issue. The fact is, though, the couple is not fighting over toothpaste. They are fighting over his coming home late and over the glass of cold water she poured on his head.

Gunny sacking can kill a marriage. It can also kill a church, a family and a potential relationship.

One of the reasons that a lack of boldness is so horrible is not because of self-image, but because a lack of honesty simply does not allow a relationship to go any deeper than a child's wading pool.

This is the principle: If honesty and confrontation destroy a relationship, it was not worth anything, anyway. Forgiveness provides the opportunity for honesty. So, forgive easily.

Thou Shalt Affirm Quickly

The ninth commandment: Thou shalt affirm quickly.

I thank my God always concerning you for the grace of God which was given to you by Christ Jesus. (1 Corinthians 1:4)

A Christian's demeanor is always other-directed. It should be your goal, not only to be a bold, honest and confrontational Christian, but also to see others become bold, honest and confrontational.

Someone has said that the first question God will ask us when we get to heaven is this: *Who did you bring with you?* Right now, the question you should ask yourself is this: *Who became bold besides myself?*

My second most favorite thing in the world is to speak for youth rallies. (My favorite thing is jumping off twenty-story buildings!) Seriously, though, the group I'd rather talk to more than any other is those who work with young people.

I spoke for the National Convention of Youth for Christ once and, to be honest, I was great! In fact, I was even taking notes on myself! I have never spoken before a more responsive and excited group of people.

Afterward, I asked one of the leaders why it was so easy to speak for them. He said, "Steve, when you talk to youth workers, you are talking to people who stand before the hardest audience in the world—teenagers. They have bombed, have made fools of themselves and have been very afraid. Because that is true, they understand and are for you in a way that is far deeper than any other group in the world. They are your cheerleaders."

And I thought it was me . . .

It is the same way with speaking for an African American church. When I was still a pastor, my friend, Billy Baskins, and I sometimes exchanged pulpits. Billy is a black pastor of a predominately black church and I was a white pastor of a predominately white church. When Billy would preach for my congregation, he would say, "If you don't help me, we're going to be here all afternoon!"

Billy actually got the white congregation saying "Amen!" and "Praise the Lord!" with the best of them!

When I first preached at Billy's church, it was really bad. Between services, one of the deacons told me, "Pastor Brown, you said some good things; but, don't go so fast, because we want to help you."

Do you know what happened? I preached one of the best sermons of my life and covered only half the material. We had a thing going and I began to realize why black preachers are so great. It is not them; it is their congregations who become cheerleaders in the process.

One of the best rules in the book *The One Minute Manager* is to catch someone doing right and to tell them so. Likewise, catch your brothers and sisters in Christ being bold and encourage them, letting them know that you're proud of them.

I am a reasonably free person. That is sufficient for me. The only reason I'm writing this book and doing the "Born Free" seminars is so I might see you free, becoming your cheerleader in the process.

There is an interesting statement in Hebrews 12:1:

> Therefore we also, since we are surrounded by so great a cloud of witnesses, let us lay aside every weight, and the sin which so easily ensnares us, and let us run with endurance the race that is set before us.

Using athletic imagery, the writer of Hebrews is referring to a gigantic stadium where, in the stands, are the great giants of the Faith. Sometimes, in my mind's eye, I see that great cloud of witnesses cheering me on.

I can hear Moses yelling, "Great! Don't you back off one bit. It was hard for me too."

And Jeremiah, "I was so scared I cried, Steve. Keep on trucking."

And Amos, "Don't you shilly-shally."

And Rahab, "You think you are bad. I was a prostitute, but I stood and you can stand too."

You have a cheering section. Every time you stand, every time you're counted, every time you say what you think, and every time you refuse to be manipulated, someone in heaven says, "Yes! Go get 'em!"

As we receive affirmation from the Father and from the past of bold, earthy and free Christians, we need to do the same thing for our brothers and sisters in Christ.

Thou Shalt Credit Biblically

Finally, the tenth commandment of Christian boldness: Thou shalt credit biblically. What is the true source of your new-found boldness?

Every good gift and every perfect gift is from above, and comes down from the Father of lights, with whom there is no variation or shadow of turning. (James 1:17)

... giving thanks always for all things to God the Father in the name of our Lord Jesus Christ ... (Ephesians 5:20)

A final principle in this program of boldness: *God only makes you responsible for what you know and, once you know it, He will create the existential situation in which you can be responsible.*

I believe that, as a result of what you have learned in this book, God is going to put you into situations where you will need to confront, to be clear and honest, and to be bold. When you are faithful, remember who gave you the gasoline and praise Him for it.

In the second book of C. S. Lewis's science fiction trilogy, *Perelandra*, the character of Ransom, the Christ figure, has gone to a brand new planet to prevent a Fall from taking place, similar to that on earth.

The character of Weston, the personification of evil, is also on the planet. He is horrible. You can always find him by checking out the string of entrails he has ripped out of small animals or the beautiful blossoms he has ripped from their stems and crushed.

At any rate, Ransom realizes that he is to do battle, a battle to the death, with Weston. Ransom also realizes that he has a choice. All the black night, he struggles with that choice.

Then, in the silence, Ransom hears a voice. The voice says, "My name is also Ransom."[25]

Stand . . . and the Father will come. When He is there, you will know that He deserves all the praise because of the principle: *You take the first step, He will take the second step and, by the time you get to the third step, you will know that He was the one who took the first step all along.*

Just don't forget to thank Him.

8

Perseverance

Holding the Land of Boldness
and Freedom

We have come miles and miles to this point. Now, for a warning. It has to do with the law of reversion. It is this: In Christian living, passivity is the causative factor in behavioral reversion. In other words, because the bondage of prison is so natural to human beings, one must constantly be on the lookout for the danger of returning. The fact is, you have to actively hold on to the land of boldness and freedom.

In one of the stories by John Galsworthy, English novelist and playwright, there is a doctor in a mining town who has sold his soul to the company store. It didn't happen overnight. It was incremental.

When he was a young man, the doctor had been very kind and compassionate in giving of himself to the miners in the town, often without compensation. But, over the years, he had changed.

In the story, the doctor's wife dies. After her funeral, the doctor goes home. He rummages through his wife's purse and comes across some old, yellowed letters from miners who had thanked the doctor for his kindness, skill and, in many cases, free service.

The doctor, now an old man, walks over to the mirror in the living room and looks at his own image. He starts to cry and, through the sobs, the doctor says, "You thought you would get away with it, didn't you? But, by God, you didn't."

Our natures are so fallen, our bent to sin so strong and Satan so real, that, if we sit around and do nothing, we will gradually lose the ground we have achieved.

That is certainly true of being a free and bold Christian. If you take the teaching from this book and apply it, you are going to face all kinds of pressure. You are going to be criticized. You are going to be looked down on as less of a Christian. You are going to find yourself thinking of the days when you didn't make waves, when you were a phoney, when you were dishonest . . . and when you were liked by everyone.

And, as a result, there will be times when you will want to go back.

We have seen it before—Paul's surprise at the Galatians should not have been a surprise. He wrote:

> I marvel that you are turning away so soon from Him who called you in the grace of Christ, to a different gospel. (Galatians 1:6)

> Christ has redeemed us from the curse of the law, having become a curse for us . . . (Galatians 3:13)

So, before we finish, I want to offer some help in holding the land. It is very valuable land, bought with a terrible price . . . the blood of Christ. Let's check it out.

The Gurus Who Loot the Land

First, note the gurus who loot the land of freedom and boldness. They can be found in our lives, as well as throughout Scripture:

> An astonishing and horrible thing has been committed in the land: The prophets prophesy falsely, and the priests rule by their own power; and My people love to have it so. But what will you do in the end? (Jeremiah 5:30–31)

> Not that we have dominion over your faith, but are fellow workers for your joy; for by faith you stand. (2 Corinthians 1:24)

For we are not, as so many, peddling the word of God; but as of sincerity, but as from God, we speak in the sight of God in Christ. (2 Corinthians 2:17)

I urged Titus, and sent our brother with him. Did Titus take advantage of you? Did we not walk in the same spirit? Did we not walk in the same steps? (2 Corinthians 12:18)

For consider Him who endured such hostility from sinners against Himself, lest you become weary and discouraged in your souls. (Hebrews 12:3)

Do you know what really irritates me? People who take free and joyous new Christians and make them into sour, negative and judgmental Christians.

In Matthew 18, the disciples ask Jesus, "Who then is greatest in the kingdom of heaven?" In answer, Jesus takes a child and says, "Assuredly, I say to you, unless you are converted and become as little children, you will by no means enter the kingdom of heaven" (v. 3).

When Jesus talked about childlikeness, He was not talking about purity. Any parent knows that a child may be innocent, but a child isn't pure. Jesus was, I suspect, talking about smallness, trust, joy and freedom.

The interesting part of that passage is what immediately follows. Jesus says:

But whoever causes one of these little ones who believe in Me to sin, it would be better for him if a millstone were hung around his neck, and he were drowned in the depth of the sea. (v. 6)

Of course, I believe that Jesus was literally talking about little children there; but, given its juxtaposition in the text, I believe that He was also talking about those who rob Christians of their trust, joy and freedom.

It happens all the time, often for good reasons. We think that there has to be more discipline, more obedience, more holiness and more sanctification . . . and all of that is true. It is just that those things don't come from effort, they come from being free and loved.

The fact is, there are those who would rob you of your freedom. They may do it out of concern, jealousy or meanness; but, for whatever reason, don't let them.

There is a biblical doctrine called "the priesthood of all believers." That doctrine teaches, among other things, that no one can be your mother, your master or your priest, because no one is any more qualified than you are.

There are many brothers and sisters in Christ who believe that they have God in their back pockets. Allow me to let you in on a little secret: They don't.

Where did I get that information?

Do not be wise in your own eyes . . . (Proverbs 3:7)

Do you see a man wise in his own eyes? There is more hope for a fool than for him. (Proverbs 26:12)

Behold, I will make you small among the nations; you shall be greatly despised. The pride of your heart has deceived you, you who dwell in the clefts of the rock, whose habitation is high; you who say in your heart, "Who will bring me down to the ground?" Though you ascend as high as the eagle, and though you set your nest among the stars, from there I will bring you down, says the LORD. (Obadiah 2–4)

Edward Bratcher gives a wonderful prayer in his book, *The Walk on Water Syndrome*. It is a prayer that every teacher, leader and Christian celebrity ought to pray:

O Lord God, thou hast made me a pastor and teacher in the church. Thou sees how unfit I am to administer rightly this great, responsible office; and had I been without thy aid and counsel, I would surely have ruined it long ago. Therefore do I invoke thee.

How gladly do I desire to yield and consecrate my heart and mouth to this ministry. I desire to teach the congregation. I, too, desire ever to learn and to keep thy Word my constant companion and to meditate thereupon earnestly.

Use me as thy instrument in thy service. Only do not thou forsake me, for if I am left to myself, I will certainly bring it all to destruction. Amen.[26]

Freedom and boldness are gifts from God. Don't let leaders take them away from you. I have gone down a lot of wrong roads, following a lot of sincere, strong, articulate . . . and wrong leaders. There are three things I have learned.

First, I have learned that there are no infallible teachers or leaders. God had only one perfect preacher. His name was Jesus Christ. Be careful about everybody else, including me.

Second, I have learned that no teacher or leader should be judged on the basis of the size of the crowd, the bigness of the church, the glibness of the tongue, the sincerity of the voice, the certainty of the demeanor or the glitter of the ministry. (Hitler got a big crowd, he had a glib tongue, he was sincere and certain . . . and the Third Reich was nothing, if it didn't have glitter.)

Third, I have learned that, when authority (other than God's authority) is asked to be accepted without explanation, that authority is usually not from God.

So, watch carefully for gurus who are out to rob the land of freedom and boldness.

The Truth That Holds the Land

Second, note the truth that holds the land.

But we have renounced the hidden things of shame, not walking in craftiness nor handling the word of God deceitfully, but by manifestation of the truth . . . (2 Corinthians 4:2)

All Scripture is given by inspiration of God, and is profitable for doctrine, for reproof, for correction, for instruction in righteousness, that the man of God may be complete, thoroughly equipped for every good work. (2 Timothy 3:16–17)

If this book on living free teaches you anything, I hope it teaches you to see the Bible in a new light. When you have been in the prison long enough, you begin to see everything in terms of the prison. Every verse of the Bible becomes another condemnation. Every admonishment specifically applies to you. Every sin becomes your sin. Every statement about freedom, love and acceptance applies to someone else.

It is an old story, but a good one. A psychiatrist is giving the inkblot test to one of his patients. (The inkblot test is one in which the patient is asked to tell the therapist what he or she sees in various black images which have no form or content.)

At any rate, after each inkblot, the patient described an erotic or pornographic picture. Finally, the psychiatrist, astounded that the patient would be that consistent, said, "Sir, do you mean that you see something sexual in every one of these pictures?"

"Look, doc," the patient replied, "I'm not the one with the dirty pictures!"

When you study the Scripture, pray that you will receive the "whole counsel of God." Know what your Bible says. When someone claims . . .

> . . . that you must not be a real Christian
>
> . . . that Christians don't do what you're doing
>
> . . . that you can never be used
>
> . . . that you are dirty and horrible
>
> . . . that God cannot understand
>
> . . . that every bad thing which happens to you is because of God's punishment

. . . know the truth of what the Bible really teaches.

In other words, read those portions of the Bible which you didn't underline.

The Values That Define the Land

Third, note the values that define the land.

> I will bless the LORD who has given me counsel; my heart also instructs me in the night seasons. I have set the LORD always before me; because He is at my right hand I shall not be moved. Therefore my heart is glad, and my glory rejoices; my flesh also will rest in hope. (Psalm 16:7–9)

Fred Smith, who is given to the shock value of words, often says, "God loves you, but He doesn't have a wonderful plan for your life."

So many Christians are simply ego-centered. They actually think that they must determine what God's will is for the color of the house in which they live!

The Bible teaches that there are certain things you should never do—like murder, commit adultery, lie, cheat and steal. The Bible also teaches that there are certain things you should always do—like show love and compassion, forgive and be honest. *Outside of those, you are free.*

Now that puts a lot of responsibility on you. God has given each person twenty-four hours in a day. God has given each person a mind. And, finally, God has given each Christian the Spirit of Christ. Ask the Lord to give you a list of the values in your life to which He has called you. Then, after prayerful consideration, determine your actions by that list of values.

For example, I have, after due consideration and prayer, decided that God has called me to be a teacher of biblical principles. Because that is true, I have learned to say "no" to all of those concerns which don't lend themselves to that particular value.

A number of years ago, I was asked to become the president of a prominent seminary. It was so wild and so much from left-field,

I thought that maybe it came from God. This seminary was in trouble and I knew why they wanted me to be the president . . . even if they didn't.

I have a mean streak and I was sure that I would be the president just long enough to fire a number of people, to clean house and to set up the standard. Then, they would get somebody else. I would, in effect, become a "sacrificial lamb."

Nevertheless, I was willing to become president if that was what God wanted for my life. At the time, Anna and I traveled to a conference where I was speaking, not knowing what to do about the request to become president of this seminary. I took two letters with me. One accepted the offer and the other withdrew my name. To be honest with you, I was in agony over the whole situation.

My friend, Rusty Anderson, somehow heard about the offer. He didn't know where I was; but, finally, he tracked me down at the hotel. The phone rang in our room. Rusty didn't engage in small talk. In fact, he didn't even say "hello."

I picked up the phone and Rusty said, "Brown, who told you that you were smart enough to be a seminary president? Are you crazy? God didn't call you to do that. Do you want to be miserable the rest of your life?"

After our phone conversation, I mailed the letter, withdrawing my name from consideration.

What's the point? Decide what you are about (a mother, a teacher, a business person, a ball player, a preacher, a candlestick maker, a writer) and learn to gauge your time. Say "no" to those things which do not enhance or further the fulfillment of those values. Evaluate your life by your values and learn to say "no" to that which is not the place to which God has called you.

Once you know, in your freedom, what land to occupy, refuse to occupy other people's land. When you know who you are and what you are to do, it is a tremendous defense against those who would attempt to manipulate and control you.

The Rewards That Sell the Land

Fourth, note the rewards that sell the land.

> But when the fullness of the time had come, God sent forth His Son, born of a woman, born under the law, to redeem those who were under the law, that we might receive the adoption as sons. And because you are sons, God has sent forth the Spirit of His Son into your hearts, crying out, "Abba, Father!" Therefore you are no longer a slave but a son, and if a son, then an heir of God through Christ. (Galatians 4:4–7)

I have an aversion to "Prosperity Theology." I just can't see how things could be so good for the followers of a religion whose founder ended up on a cross and whose chief spokesman had a physical problem that God wouldn't remove (2 Corinthians 12).

However, freedom costs . . . but freedom also carries its rewards. Remember the rewards. It will help you hold the land.

- The free Christian finds that he or she is living a life of progressive sanctification; not because he or she has to, but because of a joyous response to love.
- The free Christian is released from the demons of the past and is no longer enslaved to the heritage of the prison.
- The free Christian is free from a life of rules. "Thou shalt not" is not the basis of a relationship with God.
- The free Christian is no longer living in constant fear of other people, of being discovered, of failing or of making a mistake.
- The free Christian is no longer haunted by an overwhelming sense of guilt. Guilt is replaced by the realization of being acceptable to God.
- The free Christian is shed of empty religion, of meaningless acts of piety. He or she doesn't have to pretend to be a Christian anymore.

- The free Christian is released from the social pressure to be something or to do something.
- The free Christian is released from the need to whine about being a worm. He or she can now accept compliments and praise without feeling guilty.
- The free Christian can accept his or her humanness.
- The free Christian is free from the obligation to fix everything that is broken, from solving every problem and from being everybody's mother.
- The free Christian is released from the prison of failure. All of the false Christianity that made failure an asset is gone ... and the free Christian can now be everything God intended.
- And finally, the free Christian is no longer subservient to false heroes or to manipulative gurus.

One time, a young woman told my associate and friend, Dave O'Dowd, "Dave, I have never hurt so much as I have since becoming a Christian. I cry where I didn't cry before. I am aware of stuff in me that I don't like. And I have a list of things to do that I never before thought was important."

Dave asked, "Would you rather not have known Him?"

She replied, "Oh no, He is worth it all."

He is, you know. With Him, there is real freedom and boldness in life.

Here is an important point: *Freedom is attractive to pagans.* Most people become Christians despite Christians. But, if pagans saw the freedom, they would be drawn to the Man who has the key. His name is Jesus.

The Community That Shares the Land

Fifth and finally, note the community that shares the land.

Brethren, if a man is overtaken in any trespass, you who are spiritual restore such a one in a spirit of gentleness, considering yourself lest you also be tempted. Bear one another's burdens, and so fulfill the law of Christ. For if anyone thinks himself to be something, when he is nothing, he deceives himself. But let each one examine his own work, and then he will have rejoicing in himself alone, and not in another. For each one shall bear his own load. (Galatians 6:1–5)

Let me tell you something. There is a fellowship of the free around this country and you will start seeing it everywhere.

One of the principles by which I live is this: *If you have a vision from God and you are the only one, it probably didn't come from God.*

When I wrote my book on freedom, *When Being Good Isn't Good Enough*, I received a fairly good bunch of criticism. In fact, I began to think that what I wrote in the book and what I taught in conferences and rallies was not true. I remember praying one night during that time, "Lord, have I missed it? Am I leading Christians astray? If you want, I will recant."

The very next day, after I had spoken the last time at a conference, a man I had never met came up to me and said, "Steve, I've really enjoyed what you've been teaching this week, but it isn't new to me. There is another man who is teaching the same thing."

I asked who the man was. He said, "I was at a conference three months ago. Jack Miller in Philadelphia is saying the same things you are."

When he noticed the tears welling up in my eyes, the man looked at me kind-of funny. Unknowingly, he was God's answer to my prayer. There is no man in America I respect more than Jack Miller of World Harvest and former professor at Westminster Theological Seminary. Through some very difficult times, Jack's witness has been sterling. He is a man who loves God with all of his heart.

In your new-found freedom and boldness, you are not alone. Across the church, Christians are discovering the ways to get out of the prison. You can hear them laugh in the strangest places.

When you find them, you will share the secret . . .

The laughter of the redeemed will echo and those who are still in prison will wonder what's so funny.

Your responsibility will be to tell them.

A Declaration of Independence

One time Corrie ten Boom told me, after I had expressed shock about something she'd said, "Stephen, when you are an old lady, you can say anything." I suspect that she had not waited until she was an old lady before she expressed clearly and strongly whatever she felt God wanted her to say. It was just easier as she got older.

You don't have to wait either. And that is what this book has been about: Living out freedom and boldness. If you have read thus far, to this final chapter, let me compliment you. Given the fact that I have someplace in these pages offended almost everyone, you are either a heathen worshiper of the Greek goddess Athena or you are the kind of Christian who is tired of being forced into anybody's mold . . . that is, except God's.

In Martin Bell's delightful book, *The Way of the Wolf*, he presents biblical truths in images that create fresh ways to think of Christ. In one of the chapters, there is the story of a little boy who traveled with a wolf out of the warmth and safety of the forest. The story whispers of the Incarnation: The silver wolf is God; the little boy who loses his magic, Jesus; and the wind, the Holy Spirit. The story concerns the boy who lost the silver wolf (his magic), got murdered and then got the magic back. Bell writes:

> The boy stood quietly with his arms relaxed. There, barely discernible on a path leading out of the forest, was the silver wolf. Neither of them moved.
>
> "How much longer can we wait?" asked the boy.
>
> The wolf did not answer. He seemed to be sensing after something in the air. His powerful body was absolutely motionless.
>
> "I'm not at all sure that I like this," the boy went on, "Everything is so—well, so different! Even you don't know what it's going to be like there. Or what is going to happen to us. Maybe we shouldn't go. Have you ever thought about that? About not going, I mean?"

The wolf was silent.

"How much longer can we wait?" asked the boy. There was no reply.

Then suddenly, wind. The silver wolf's fur stood on end. The boy shielded his eyes. Dead leaves swirled and scattered about his feet. The trees themselves seemed to be leaning over to touch him.

Now apparently the wolf was satisfied. He still didn't speak. Nor did he change his expression. But his muscles went slack and he turned completely around. For one desperate moment the boy thought of running away. But that moment ended, and then the three of them were headed down the path that led out of the forest. The silver wolf. The wind. And the boy who was soon to lose his magic.[27]

Christians who have decided to be bold, free Christians are a lot like the little boy who was about to lose his magic. We, too, stand on the edge of our warm forest home, knowing that the silver wolf is going to lead us into dangerous, unknown and frightening places. Of course, we are not going to lose our magic. We never had any. But it is, nevertheless, frightening. But there is more than the fear. There is the realization that we were created in the image of God, and . . .

> . . . whenever we become less than what He meant us to be,
>
> . . . whenever we allow ourselves to be manipulated,
>
> . . . whenever we engage in mindless submission either to the world or to other Christians,
>
> . . . whenever we universalize someone else's experience and try to make it our own,
>
> . . . whenever we refuse to laugh or to speak or to weep because we are afraid of what "they" will say,
>
> . . . whenever we allow guilt or fear or worry to be the primary motivating factors in our lives,
>
> . . . whenever we define humility, love or servanthood in a way other than God's way,

. . . whenever we quit thinking and feeling,

. . . whenever we allow ourselves to be bound up in tradition,

. . . whenever we bow to any other God than the One who created us

. . . we have somehow betrayed that image.

Christ has made you free. Now go out and live like it!

Notes

1. Aram Bakshian, Jr., "Gone with the Wimp," *National Review,* September 20, 1985, p. 50.

2. Calvin Miller, *The Singer* (Downers Grove, Ill.: InterVarsity Press, 1978), pp. 75–7.

3. Thomas R. Kelly, *A Testament of Devotion* (New York: Harper and Row, 1941), pp. 64–5.

4. William Kirk Kilpatrick, *Psychological Seduction* (Nashville, Tenn.: Thomas Nelson, 1985), p. 97.

5. Jones, Leisy, and Ludwig, eds., *Major American Writers* (New York: Harcourt, Brace and Co., 1952), p. 1256.

6. John Foxe, *Foxe's Christian Martyrs of the World* (Chicago: Moody Press, n.d.), p. 502.

7. Fant and Pinson, *Twenty Centuries of Great Preaching* (Waco, Tex.: Word Books, 1971), II, p. 193.

8. Quoted in James McGraw's *Great Evangelical Preachers of Yesterday* (Nashville, Tenn.: Abingdon Press, 1961), p. 40.

9. Kelly, pp. 108–9.

10. C. S. Lewis, *The Weight of Glory* (Grand Rapids, Mich.: William B. Eerdmans Pub. Co., 1949), p. 65.

11. David R. Mains, *The Rise of the Religion of Antichristism* (Grand Rapids, Mich.: Zondervan Books, 1985), p. 17.

12. "Augustine" in *Great Books of the Western World*, ed. Robert Maynard Hutchins (Chicago: Encyclopaedia Britannica, Inc., 1952), 18, p. 130.

13. Fant and Pinson, *Twenty Centuries of Great Preaching* (Waco, Tex.: Word Books, 1971), I, p. 145.

14. Quoted in Paul Tournier's *Guilt and Grace* (New York: Harper and Row, 1962), p. 70.

15. Anderson and Wilcox, eds., *A Funny Thing Happened on the Way to Church* (St. Louis, Mo.: Concordia Pub. House, 1981), p. 54.

16. Frederick Buechner, *The Sacred Journey* (San Francisco: Harper and Row, 1982), p. 45.

17. Ibid., p. 46.

18. C. S. Lewis, *Mere Christianity* (New York: Macmillan Pub. Co., 1952), p. 167.

19. Tournier, p. 70.

20. Jean Shepherd, "The Decline and Fall of the Wimp," *The Reader's Digest*, Dec. 1985 (condensed from *The Newsday Magazine*), p. 120.

21. Bill Bryson, *The Book of Blunders* (New York: Dell Publishing Co., 1982), pp. 58–9.

22. Paul Brand and Philip Yancey, *In His Image* (Grand Rapids, Mich.: Zondervan Pub. House, 1984), p. 127.

23. Quoted anonymously in the newsletter of the National Foundation for the Study of Religion and Economics, September/October 1985.

24. Benedicta Ward, trans., *The Desert Christian: The Sayings of the Desert Fathers* (New York: Macmillan Publishing Co., 1975), p. 230.

25. C. S. Lewis, *Perelandra* (New York: Macmillan Publishing Co., 1965), p. 148.

26. Edward B. Bratcher, *The Walk on Water Syndrome* (Waco, Tex.: Word Books, 1984).

27. Martin Bell, *The Way of the Wolf* (New York: Ballantine Books, 1970), pp. 67–8.

Scripture Index

Genesis

1:27   67
4:21   95

Exodus

34:10   81

Joshua

1:2-6   81
24:15   29

1 Samuel

3:20   81

2 Samuel

5:10   82
6:5   95

1 Kings

18:27   82

Psalms

16:7–9   175
34:4   132
103:14   58
111:10   132
139:23   16
150:3–4   95

Proverbs

3:7   172
23:7   16
26:12   172

Ecclesiastes

9:10   22

Jeremiah

5:30–31   170
17:9   108

Daniel

3:1–7   45–46
3:17–18   46
6:10   46

Amos

5:21–24   82

Obadiah

2-4   172

Matthew

5:37   45, 149
9:12–13   109
9:36   58
11:28–29   50
15:1–3   86
18:3   171
18:6   171
19:17   23
20:25–28   91
23:23   96
23:27–33   83
25   20
25:24–25   122
26:36–39   143

Mark

4:35–41   124
4:37–38   126
4:39   128

Luke

6:26   65
14:28–29   131
14:28–31   157
14:31–32   131
22:44   143
23:46   144

John

1:12   57
2   80
2:13–25   49
11:1–6   19
11:20–21   19
11:32   19
15:15   147

Acts

4:13   78
5:19   31
5:27–29   151
10:13–15   62
13:13   63
15:37–39   63
15:39   68
17:11   66
26:19   158

Romans

5:6-8   108
5:20   116–17
7:24   102
8:1   74
8:35–39   128
11:36   56
12:2   16, 158

1 Corinthians

1:4   163
2:2–5   58
2:3   161
3:9   153
4:3   76
9:1–6   57
9:3–5   66
12:4–31   22
16:17   154

185